Make the Leap

Think better. Train better. *Run faster*.

By Bryan Green

Praise for Make the Leap

Coaches

"If *Make the Leap* had been available I would have strongly encouraged my athletes and my assistant coaches to read it at the start of each season." Bob Larsen, 4x NCAA Coach of the Year, UCLA, Retired; 2004 US Olympic Distance Coach, Head Toad

"*Make the Leap* will transform how you think about your training, which in turn will transform your entire running experience. If you feel you have untapped potential, read this book." Matt Fitzgerald, Coach, Author of *80/20 Running* and *Chasing the Dream*

"A must-read book for athletes and coaches everywhere, a literal how-to of goals, attitude, and mindset to make better runners." Martin Dugard, Cross Country Coach and New York Times #1 bestselling author

"*Make the Leap* by Bryan Green is one of those books that every runner and coach should have in the library. Along with *Once a Runner*, *Pre*, Joe Vigil's *Road to the Top*, *Daniels' Running Formula*, *Running with the Buffaloes* and *Bowerman and the Men of Oregon*, *Make the Leap* will be one of those dog-eared books that is read, underlined, quoted, and reread." Ken Reeves, 11x CA State Cross Country Champion at Nordhoff High School

"An easy to use framework for improving your mental skills, honing a growth mindset, and achieving your potential." Jason Fitzgerald, Strength Running head coach; Host, Strength Running Podcast

"An excellent resource for runners and coaches...applicable to all areas of life: athletic, professional, and personal." Walt Lange, 9x CA State Cross Country Champion at Jesuit High School

"...The first singular, "must-have" resource for the bookshelves of all endurance athletes and coaches." Scott Abbott, Executive Director, Sacramento Running Association

Athletes

"[It] will help get you to the next level. I highly recommend his book, *Make the Leap*." Meb Keflezighi, Olympic marathon silver medalist, Boston and New York City Marathon champion

"I truly believe reading this was one of the best things I could do for myself in striving for my athletic potential." Sarah Turner, Coach/Dietician, BananasAndSplits.com

"Bryan Green accepts the 'how' and 'when' but provides the definitive 'why.'" Steve Moneghetti, Olympian, Commonwealth Games Champion

"Break free of the mental barriers...*Make the Leap* will show you the way." Jon Rankin, 3:52 miler, US Olympic 1500m alternate

"*Make the Leap* will help runners prioritize what's important in their training." Christian Cushing-murray, 3:55 miler, Masters M45 1500m record holder, Century High coach

"*Make the Leap* will have a profound and tangible impact and may just change your life." Jim Ortiz, former UCLA Cross Country Captain, Executive Recruiter

Read more at maketheleapbook.com/praise

*To Rika, for pushing me to be
the best version of myself I can be.*

*To Arisa and Reina, I can't wait
to see the amazing leaps you will make.*

Make the Leap

Diagrams/Illustrations by Bryan Green
Cover Design by Nadine Denten (@nadineinjapan)

maketheleapbook.com
maketheleapbook@gmail.com
@maketheleapbook

Contents

Foreword

If you are determined to max your potential, you need to read this book.

I coached the author of *Make the Leap*, Bryan Green, at UCLA in the late 1990s. Bryan displayed a curious intellect about effective training and what it took to be successful. He was talented but had to learn to adjust to older, even more talented teammates. As he went through that process, it sparked a desire to get better at every aspect of his life, which continues to this day.

Make the Leap is a culmination of everything Bryan learned in athletics and in a life of varied experiences. It starts with "Think Better. Train Better." Throughout my career, I always found that mental preparation was the key to my athletes' success. From doing the right workouts to executing in races to making good life choices, it all starts in your head. I put a lot of my emphasis on this as a coach.

This book will make you a better runner because it will help you think better about every part of your training. You will do each workout with more purpose. You will prepare better for your competitions. And you will see clearly what Bryan calls the "hidden training program." The result is you will max your potential and make a leap.

But this book is much more than about training. *Make the Leap* is a blueprint for living your life at a more productive level. Reading this book will help you get more out of each day. Bryan uses the latest psychological studies to explain why we come up short of our goals, and how to change our routines and habits to increase our energy levels to achieve more. You will be motivated to plan and prioritize your thoughts and actions to operate at your highest level.

If this book was available when I was coaching, I would have strongly recommended my athletes and my assistant coaches to read it at the start of each season and refer back to it when they hit a difficult patch in training, in school, or in life in general.

The great athletes I've had the good fortune to coach all had many of the attributes listed in this book. Meb, who had the longest career at the top, had them all.

I learned a lot of useful ideas from Bryan's book about staying motivated and focused on what's important in life. I am confident you will have the same experience.

Bob Larsen
Four-time NCAA Coach of the Year at UCLA, Retired
Olympic Distance Coach - Athens 2004
National Track and Field Hall of Fame
Head Toad
Brentwood, CA
August 2020

Introduction

There are countless running books that give you training programs, workout templates, and conversion tables. Others are filled with heartwarming stories and philosophical quotes.

This is not one of those books.

This book focuses on the most important aspect of running that nobody seems to talk about: how to think about training. Everyday countless runners put in the work to get better and yet they unknowingly hold themselves back. It's not the workouts! It's our approach to them.

I assume you've got the physical part of training covered. I want to help you improve the mental part.

Mental Training Matters

This book is based on one simple premise: the better we think about our training, the better we will train. *Think better, train better.*

Our brains are prediction factories, and our expectations are their outputs. We input raw materials: future goals, prior experiences, belief in our abilities, cognitive biases, enjoyment, doubt, responsibility, fear, motivation, and concentration. We turn the dial to some point in the future, the end of the season or next weekend's race. Then *whirrr*: out comes a shiny new expectation.

We create expectations about literally everything: the weather, the food we eat, other people, the news, the latest films, and everything in between. We get some new info, turn the dial and *whirrr* goes the factory.

This *whirrr* occurs in our training, too. We set expectations about what we will do, how it will feel, how important it is, what others will do, what our coaches think, what our coaches think we think. The minute you think about an aspect of your training, you've already formed an expectation about it.

So why does this matter? *Because our expectations set the ceiling for our achievement.*

> ## "Our expectations set the ceiling for our achievement."

Our expectations guide how we train. How hard we work. How anxious, stressed, or excited we feel. How much we prepare. How much (and how) we analyze our performance. How we interpret success or failure and how we structure our days around our training program. Expectations influence everything.

As dedicated runners, we put in countless hours of hard work. We can't let our expectations limit our potential. We need a mental framework that ensures our expectations are guiding us toward excellence.

I will give you that mental framework.

Naive Beginnings (Running Without Expectations)

I was always a talented runner. Running came easy to me and I enjoyed it. Over three years in high school I set a bunch of school records, won some league championships, and got noticed by colleges.

But my success masked a bigger failure: I didn't improve much over those three years. I was "the best in school history" after one year, improved a little the next year, and then stalled out there.

The reality is my mental frameworks for learning and training were broken. The way I thought held me back.

The clearest example: I did all of my runs with my shoes untied. For three years! I decided that tying shoes was a waste of time (in general) and I treated practice just like the rest of the day. If we weren't doing intervals, I just ran at "untied shoes" pace and called it a day.

I share that story because it seems so colossally dumb now. But I wasn't a dumb kid. I did great in school, picked up new concepts quickly, did well in sports, and got along well with everyone. I seemed to have it all figured out, and yet I so clearly didn't.

The truth is, school and sports came *too easy* to me. I developed a mindset that my talent determined my success. For me, the challenge was the opposite: to succeed while putting in as little effort as possible. That was the best way to demonstrate how talented I was. I thought it made me look better if I won despite never tying my shoes.[1]

I eventually walked-on at UCLA. When Bob Larsen[2] called me and said he would have a spot for me, I signed right up. I knew next to nothing about his or the program's storied history, just

---

[1] I don't blame my coaches or high school program for this. I love my coaches, teammates, and still cherish the entire experience. I had so much fun! But looking back, I definitely did not have the right mindset about training.

[2] The head coach at UCLA my first three years, and Mebrahtom (Meb) Keflezighi's long-time coach. He had a good career.

that they had Meb Keflezighi,[3] who was the best collegiate runner in the country.

My first run with the team was a wake-up call. Guys were talking about their summer training, and many had run 100 miles per week. I had done my typical summer training of…lightly jogging occasionally. The workout that day was a 9-mile tempo run. Nine miles was the farthest I'd ever run in my life. Meb and some other guys were running between 5:00 to 5:15 mile pace. That was my 3-mile race pace. (Gulp.)

As we walked to the start one of the guys said, "You gonna tie your shoes?"

I played it cool. "Oh…yeah, haha." I laced them up. I felt way way way out of my league. And yes, that first run was a debacle. But I survived and learned my first two lessons. College runners run a lot and serious runners tie their shoes.

I spent my first year injured. The following two years I was a solid contributor. I made the traveling squads. I finished seventh at the PAC-10 Championships 10,000 meters. In cross country, my best finish at the NCAA Western Regional Cross Country championships was in the high 40s.

I wanted badly to be better, but I struggled to reconcile two competing ideas. I still believed performance was a reflection of talent. I trained everyday with national champions like Meb Keflezighi, Mark Hauser,[4] and Jesse Strutzel,[5] who did workouts I couldn't dream of doing.[6] The rest of us were a couple levels below them and we accepted that as our reality.

---

[3] Winner of Boston and NYC Marathons, Olympic Silver Medalist, former American Record holder at 10,000m, 4xNCAA Champion. Among many other accomplishments. His Bio: https://marathonmeb.com/meb-keflezighi/

[4] Sub-4 miler, Mark anchored the 1999 American Record NCAA Championship distance medley relay team.

[5] 2000 NCAA Indoor 800m champ, ran 1:45, ran 1200m leg of 1999 American Record NCAA Championship distance medley relay team. Changed his name to Jesse Warren.

[6] I still remember watching Mark Hauser run a 4:00 mile…in practice…in his 4th mile repeat! It was thrilling, even as I was struggling to finish my 4th repeat some 150 meters behind!

On the other hand, there were guys I beat in high school who had made a leap and were better than me. A couple were even competitive with Mark and Jesse. I didn't believe they were more talented than me. But if not, why wasn't I running at their level?

What I didn't know, what I couldn't really conceive at the time, is that despite how hard I was working, I wasn't getting anywhere close to 100% out of myself.

By the end of my third year, I was trying to set higher expectations for myself. But I still had one problem. I didn't believe in them.

A Better Prediction Factory

The idea of our brain as a prediction factory is what's called a mental model. A mental model is a way of simplifying real world situations to better understand them.

We all know how factories work. We can use that concept to better understand how our brains create expectations.

If you want to improve the product made at a factory, you have a few options: improve the machinery, improve your processes, or get better materials. In the context of expectation-setting, you can improve brain health, improve the way you process information and make decisions, or input better thoughts and beliefs.

Let's start with brain health. If you are too tired, undernourished, dehydrated, over-stressed, and consistently distracted it puts a large strain on your brain. Part of keeping any factory running smoothly is keeping up with the maintenance. The same applies to how you think.

The way we process information and make decisions is our main focus. Some machines make higher quality widgets than other machines. Similarly, some thought processes result in better outcomes. Part of making better expectations is having the right mental frameworks for understanding the world and knowing when to use them.

But having the right frameworks in place isn't enough. How we use them is equally important. When do we turn them on and off? How do they connect with each other? What are we doing to calibrate them? We need effective processes and systems in place to ensure we get the most out of ourselves.

Lastly, we can input better thoughts and beliefs. You can't source crap materials and use them to create a luxury product. No matter how much you try, the result will be obvious. The same goes for our approach to training. If you input flawed ideas and unproductive beliefs into your head, you will produce unproductive expectations.

Here is the good news. We have a lot of influence over all three of these areas. We can live healthy lifestyles that keep our brains well maintained. We can gain a better understanding of how the world works, how our brains work, and how our thoughts tie into our real world results. And we can cultivate productive thoughts and quickly identify unproductive ones.

When we create habits and systems around all of these areas, we build high quality expectations into the core of our training routine. The improvement that follows can be almost immediate.

My First Leap

The spring of my third year I enrolled in Education 80, a course focused on the college experience.[7] It was my first introduction to social psychology and the theory of learning and achievement.

The class changed my life. It introduced me to frameworks and concepts to better understand my own performance, both in the class and on the track. I took many more courses in these areas and have pursued a lifelong interest in learning and achievement theory.

---

[7] I will always be thankful to my teammate Scott Abbott who recommended the course to me.

The principles, frameworks and mental models I learned in those courses forced me to challenge my assumptions.[8] The way I described it to a friend at the time was feeling like Neo in *The Matrix* when he sees walls of 1s and 0s and intuitively understands how the Matrix works. I felt similarly empowered (minus the cool visuals).

I made a few changes:

- I reframed my understanding of ability and potential, which raised my expectations
- I identified and corrected key negative habits and thought processes, and
- I began to appreciate the relationship between engaging in a subject and developing mastery and expertise

I have to note here: I was not discussing this with my coaches.[9] I was still doing the same workouts, just thinking about them differently. And then making better decisions about how I spent my time outside of practice.

The improvements in my running were immediate. I made a dramatic leap. My junior year I finished in the top ten in every cross country race, and qualified for the NCAA Championships as an individual. I then dropped over a minute in the 10k and finished 3rd at the PAC-10 Championships.

I also saw remarkable improvement in my studies. I put the same amount of effort into my classes, but my grades went up and my learning increased. This was all a bonus for me, as I wasn't focused on my academics at the time. But I noticed it happening, and I could tell the two were related.

My senior year was tougher. I had injuries, illnesses, and my father passed away after prolonged health problems. But despite it all, I won my first (and only) collegiate cross country meet and

---

[8] The Optimal Training Principles were initially derived from the PALS learning framework developed by Winston Doby.

[9] Coach Larsen retired that year, and was succeeded by Eric Peterson (currently Director of Cross Country and Track and Field at Tulane University) and Helen Lehman-Winters (currently the associate head coach at the University of Oregon).

I qualified again for NCAAs. I also ran close to my personal best times on the track that spring.

At the time, I felt extremely frustrated. I had expected the leap to continue. That didn't happen but I also didn't regress. I had established a new "normal."

After graduating I stopped running competitively. But I didn't stop using the mental approach that helped me to make a leap. In fact, I found it to be applicable to every area of my life.

I used it to learn two languages (Japanese and Italian). I used it to excel at graduate school. I used it to navigate complex consulting projects at Fortune 50 companies and later applied the mindset daily to excel in my career at Apple. I used it to organize international conferences and even launch a startup. I now teach these concepts at one of Japan's leading universities.

The mindset I cultivated to run faster ended up improving every aspect of my life. The more I research it, the more I find that great performers in all areas use these same principles to achieve their success. Great performers think alike.

There are two reasons why it's critical for every athlete to improve how they think about training. First, it makes you better, faster. It is the low hanging fruit of improvement. Second, adopting it in one aspect of your life will make it available to you to use anywhere. Unlike physical skills, it is universally transferrable.

Reason #1: Mental Training is Low Hanging Fruit

You may have heard the expression "low hanging fruit." The low hanging fruit is the easiest to pick from the tree. It gives the most benefit for the least effort. More bang for your buck.

Mental training–improving our prediction factories–is the low hanging fruit for aspiring athletes. Countless athletes–perhaps even you–are working hard, doing good workouts, and trying to improve. But something isn't clicking.

The workouts are not the problem. Having a better mental framework to understand training is what's missing. It doesn't matter how good the training plan is if you are holding yourself back mentally.

"It doesn't matter how good the training plan is if you are holding yourself back mentally."

Here's what happens when you train how you think. You engage more. You prioritize better. You take more responsibility. You focus on the quality of your effort. You learn better from mistakes. You train purposefully. You systematize your life. And you raise your expectations.

Any one of these improvements can lead to better workouts. The combined power of these positive changes is a profound increase in the quality of your training. And that will lead to a big leap.

Here's the best thing: you don't even need to change your workouts. The leap comes from optimizing what you're already doing.

Reason #2: Mental Training is Transferrable

This brings us to the second (and biggest) reason mental training is important: it is transferrable. Running faster and making a leap is the short-term benefit. The long-term benefit is in what thinking better will do for the rest of your life.

The physical skills and specific knowledge we get in sports rarely transfers outside the sport. They only truly get used while we do the sport.

But thinking better transfers to any field. More and more research is showing how experts in numerous fields use the same fundamental approach to succeed. You can, too.

So if these ideas apply to every field, why focus on running? Why not write a general book for a general audience? Two reasons.

First, running is special to me. My success in running, modest as it was, made me the person I am today. I want all runners to maximize their abilities and get the most out of the sport.

Second, abstract ideas are useless. Ideas have to be applied. Running provides the perfect setting to practice these concepts.

- Success is clearly defined and unambiguous
- You are already motivated to get better
- You have countless daily opportunities to test small changes, and
- Running faster is by itself worth the minimal investment you'll put in

Once you apply these ideas, you'll see immediate improvement in your running. It will validate the approach. I don't have to sell you on the long-term benefits. You will get those for free.

Setting Expectations

Here's what you can expect. Each chapter is centered around an Optimal Training Principle. There are 11 in total. These principles are core beliefs shared by champions and experts in every field. I introduce them, explain them with some details, and then give some tips for how to integrate them into your training.

The book is split into two parts. Part 1 focuses on Attitudes, Beliefs, and Values. Part 2 focuses on Effort and Behavior. Mixed in throughout are shorter chapters I call Spotlights. Here I introduce powerful ideas that I've found to be helpful in my own improvement.

I should also note: I've made a supplementary workbook[10] that includes actionable questions and activities you can do to apply the concepts in the book to your training. If you have the workbook, I recommend reviewing those questions at the end of each chapter. If not, no worries, you don't need it to make a leap.

Before we get to the Optimal Training Principles, however, let's review what it means to "make a leap." It's not just a catchy phrase. It's the natural, predictable result of a specific kind of training process.

---

[10] Available at maketheleapbook.com

1. What is a "Leap"? Understanding Feedback Loops

I sometimes wonder who made the biggest leap in the history of running. Whose improvement from one season to the next was so large that it simply defied common sense?

The biggest, most impressive leap by someone I know was made by my friend and teammate Jon Rankin.

Jon arrived at UCLA and quickly established himself as a solid 1500 meter runner. He ran 3:47 as a freshman and won the 1500 meter race at the Junior U.S. Championships. Then for the next three years, he struggled with injuries and inconsistency, and made few improvements to his personal bests. He was extremely frustrated, and considered quitting.

Jon expected to be an elite miler. But he wasn't achieving that goal. He didn't even feel he was making progress. The disconnect between his goals and his performance made him feel like a failure.

Midway through his junior year, he did a complete reset. He made a conscious effort to change the way he thought about his training. Rather than focus on his big goals, he decided to emphasize doing the work and enjoying it. He was no longer going to judge himself on his results. He would focus only on his execution.

A remarkable thing happened. A metaphorical weight was lifted and he started performing better.

By the end of his fourth year, he had lowered his 1500 meter time to 3:43, close to a 4-minute mile. He finished 4th at the PAC-10 championships. The next cross country season, he was the #1 runner and earned All-American status at the NCAA Championships. He was very good. And then he made a ginormous leap.

The following spring and summer Jon recorded 17 personal bests and lowered his 1500 meter time to 3:35 (roughly a 3:53 mile). He took four seconds off his personal best over four years, and then took another eight seconds off in one year. For someone at his level, a leap this big is practically unheard of.

Anyone, at any level, can make a leap. But the better you are, the harder it gets and the smaller the leap tends to be. There just isn't that much improvement to be made.

"Anyone, at any level, can make a leap."

Most people make a leap from average to good (this was me). Fewer make the leap from good to very good. And very few make the leap from very good to elite. Jon went from very good to the 5th fastest American and 38th fastest performer in the world that year. He leapt right over elite and went straight to world-class.

He then continued to train at a world class level for the next few years. Despite battling numerous obstacles, he maintained this form and just missed qualifying for the Olympic Games in 2008. He stopped running competitively at that time after being diagnosed with chronic kidney disease.[11]

---

[11] You can learn more about Jon at https://gobemore.co/founder.

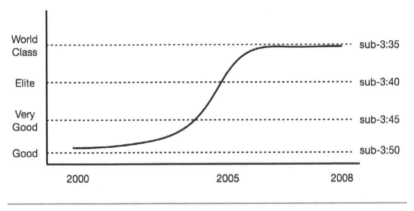

Fig 1 - Jon Rankin's leap charted on a graph

Jon's leap was rare simply because of the degree to which he improved. But if we ignore that aspect, we can see that it was structurally the same as any other leap. It started with a long period of gradual improvement, then his improvement shot up before plateauing again at a new (much higher) level. On a graph it would look something like the chart above.

Every person who makes a leap has an improvement curve that looks like this one. The labels are different, but the general shape is the same. Let's break down exactly how this type of improvement happens.

It starts with understanding feedback loops.

Feedback Loops are Fundamental

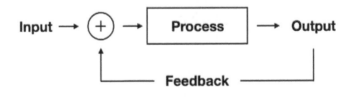

Fig 2 - A view of a feedback loop that isolates its key components

In a feedback loop, you start with an input and run it through a process. The output then "feeds back" into the process, becoming an input. You can diagram it like the previous chart.

You may have heard of this by another name. We sometimes refer to positive feedback loops as *virtuous cycles* and negative feedback loops as *vicious cycles*. Customer reviews are a simple example of how one system can generate both. Five-star reviews help generate more business, whereas one-star reviews reduce future business.

Our training is a feedback loop. The input is our current ability. The process is our training program. The output is our ability post-training. If you are continuously improving, then the process starts with a slightly improved "you" each day.

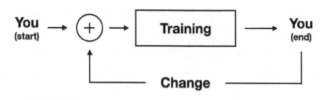

Fig 3 - In a training program, training is the process and the feedback is your improvement at the end of the training period

Let's really make this concrete and break down the main components individually.

You: You are both the Input and the Output of your training program. But "You" consist of more than just your physical body. "You" includes also how you think and feel. There is a huge difference between starting your training feeling healthy, energetic and confident versus feeling broken down, tired and dispirited. Part of maintaining a positive feedback loop is *feeling positive*.

Training: Training does not equal workouts. Our workouts are just a part of our training. There is much more we need to do. I call this the Hidden Training Program: *everything you really need to do to be successful*. The Hidden Training Program includes your diet, sleep, living situation, social activities, work, and studies, as well as your formal training program.[12]

Change: Change can be positive, negative, or neutral. If you injure yourself, it's negative. If you get better, it's positive. In a short time frame–like one day–it can be hard to see any change.

Time: We can view our training feedback loop from any time frame. We typically think in terms of seasons and years when we want to track our overall development. We think in weeks when we want to analyze our training program. And we think in days when we want to focus on building better habits.

Your actual feedback loop is impossible to calculate, especially at the daily level. We have no idea what percent of yesterday's improvement is fed back into today.

That's fine. It's more important to understand this conceptually, because it's fundamental to understanding how leaps are made.

Put simply, the goal is to wake up every morning retaining as much of your previous improvement as possible. That way your training begins to compound on itself.

Improvement Doesn't Follow a Straight Line

We are primed by our daily experience to think in linear terms. A little effort here leads to a little improvement there. And if we just keep doing what we are doing, we'll eventually get where we want to go.

Here's a simple example:
- If I put my spare change in a jar every day, after one day I'll have a small amount
- After one month I'll have roughly 30 times as much change
- After one year I'll have roughly 365 times as much change

---

[12] We'll cover this in detail when we discuss Engagement.

The growth looks like a straight line. And this makes sense to us. In fact, I'd argue that most people mistakenly think of their training this way: "If I just bank each day's workout, consistent improvement is sure to follow." I know that's how I thought about training when I first started.

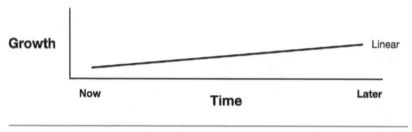

Fig 4 - We tend to think of growth and improvement as progressing linearly

In this way of thinking, feedback loops don't matter. Our quality—how well we improve—doesn't change. We have to do more to get more.

Many things in the world are linear, but not all. There are some areas that grow exponentially, for example compound interest (i.e. credit card debt), technology adoption, rabbit populations, and our ability to learn. These systems compound over time, meaning continuous small changes accumulate over time to create dramatic future change.

It is easiest to explain this using money. Imagine two people each invest $1,000 every year and get 10% interest. Each get paid $100 at the end of the year. Person A takes the money and spends it on nice dinners. Person B reinvests the money. The following table outlines how their relative investments change over time.

After one year, there is no difference between the two. After five years, the difference is hardly noticeable. After 10 years we are starting to see a slight gap. But you could easily argue that the enjoyment Person A gets from spending the cash is worth it.

It isn't until we get way out into the future that we can start to see the real differences. After 25 years Person B will have almost

Person A		1 Year	2 Years	5 Years	10 Years	25 Years	50 Years
	Principal	$1,000	$2,000	$5,000	$10,000	$25,000	$50,000
	New Investment	$1,000	$1,000	$1,000	$1,000	$1,000	$1,000
	Interest Re-invested	$0	$0	$0	$0	$0	$0
	Total Principal	$2,000	$3,000	$6,000	$11,000	$26,000	$51,000
	Cash Spent (Cumulative)	$100	$300	$1,500	$6,600	$35,100	$132,600
	Total Principal + Cash	**$2,100**	**$3,300**	**$7,500**	**$17,600**	**$61,100**	**$183,600**
Person B	Principal	$1,000	$2,100	$6,105	$15,937	$98,347	$1,163,908
	New Investment	$1,000	$1,000	$1,000	$1,000	$1,000	$1,000
	Interest Re-invested	$100	$210	$611	$1,594	$9,835	$116,391
	Total Principal	$2,100	$3,310	$7,716	$18,531	$109,182	$1,281,299
	Cash Spent (Cumulative)	$0	$0	$0	$0	$0	$0
	Total Principal + Cash	**$2,100**	**$3,310**	**$7,716**	**$18,531**	**$109,182**	**$1,281,299**
	Person B Increased Earnings	**$0**	**$10**	**$216**	**$931**	**$48,082**	**$1,097,699**

Fig 5 - The longer we allow compounding to continue, the larger the difference becomes (side note: start saving now!)

$50k more money, and after 50 years Person B will have over $1 million more in the bank.

This image shows what exponential growth looks like visually. The two lines follow a similar trajectory for some time. Early on, even exponential growth looks linear. But after they diverge the gap gets bigger and bigger.

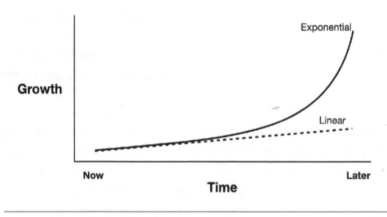

Fig 6 - Linear and Exponential growth look similar for a long time (but they are not!)

This same concept applies to training. Imagine instead of years that we are talking about weeks of training. The more of each week's improvement you retain, the faster you will arrive at the inflection point where your improvement starts to go vertical.

Here's the thing: in the beginning, you don't see any difference! When forced with the decision to eat healthy or eat junk, you will rarely notice any difference tomorrow. It takes a long-term perspective to understand that eating healthy food is like reinvesting your interest. Eating healthy food everyday creates an opportunity for us to compound the benefits. Likewise, eating junk food is like taking the cash and having fun with it. The same applies for extra stretching, treatment, sleep, etc.

Or consider stopping a great workout while you still feel great. How many of us push too hard when we feel great simply *because* we feel great that day? We feel like we've got that cash in our hand so we just spend it.

I remember a teammate was late for lunch one Sunday because he ran 27 miles that morning. He was scheduled to run 18 but was feeling great so he decided to just run a full marathon distance, something he'd never done before.

You only do this if you view training as a linear process. 27 miles is better than 18 because doing more gets you more. But his legs were sore and tired the next day (understandably) and while I can't prove it, I would bet those extra miles hurt him more than they helped.

One great workout doesn't make you a champion. One hundred great workouts won't either. It could take thousands before you are even close.

When you understand that improvement is not linear, and that positive feedback loops lead to compounding improvement, you behave differently. You focus on quality work and feeling good. You don't look for dramatic improvement today. You train knowing the big improvement will come in the future.

The Limits of Our Potential

I bet you're asking, "How can training be exponential when we obviously can't just improve forever?"

Training and earning money *are* different in one key respect. There is no theoretical limit to how much money we can have, whereas everybody has a limit on how fast they can run. We call that limit our potential.

Take the marathon. Eliud Kipchoge recently broke the two-hour barrier, which is an amazing milestone for the human race.[13] We don't know what our limit is. It could be 1:59 or it could be 1:55.

The actual limit is less important than the acknowledgment that it's there, somewhere. For our purposes, we just need to be able to draw it on a picture.

---

[13] Some would argue it's an amazing milestone for our shoe technology. There's no need to argue. It's both!

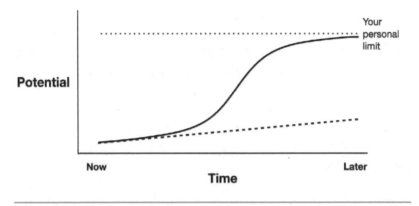

Fig 7 - The highest we can possibly leap is defined by our personal limit at that time.

Let's assume our potential is represented as an upper limit. Our improvement curve rises exponentially and then naturally bends to approach the limit. As you no doubt realized, this is *exactly the same shape* that we charted with Jon's leap earlier.

We start by creating positive feedback loops. These feedback loops lead to compounding improvement. Compounding over enough time leads to exponential improvement. The level of that exponential improvement is determined by how good the feedback loop is as well as the limits of our short-term potential.

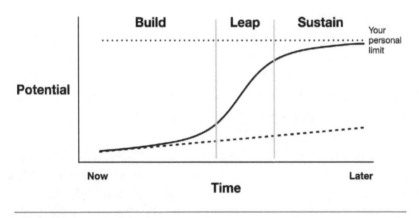

Fig 8 - Our Leap Cycle consists of 3 phases: Build, Leap, Sustain.

Breaking down the "Leap Cycle"

Now, imagine you are maintaining a positive feedback loop and setting yourself up to make a leap. Here's a breakdown of the "leap cycle":

1. Build: For some period of time, you won't see much difference. It still feels linear. This period lasts months, cannot be avoided, and is completely normal.

1-to-2. Build to Leap: Things start to feel a bit easier. You feel a little better at the end of hard workouts. You finish a little stronger at the end of some races. You aren't significantly better than before, but you're consistently performing well. Something is working.

2. Leap: You find yourself competing with people who were formerly better than you. You start blasting big PRs. You feel like a new person with new powers, but you also have some doubts because you don't know the extent of your ability. You begin systematizing many areas of your life to ensure you don't lose these new powers.

2-to-3. Leap to Sustain: You enter races knowing you are going to run well and you feel you belong at this new level. It feels like a failure to imagine a performance at your previous level. Your improvement energizes you to stay disciplined and maintain your newfound ability. You're having a lot of fun.

3. Sustain: You are reaching your upper limit. Your old training group and competitors are in the rearview mirror. So are poor performances, which you've mostly eliminated. However, you aren't seeing many improvements, despite your hard work. It starts to look and feel linear once more. Again, this cannot be avoided and is completely normal.

If you are still young and early in your career, making the leap above *does not* mean you have reached your potential. It is more likely your Sustain phase is transitioning into another Build phase prior to another leap. If you are an older veteran and have lived an optimal training lifestyle for many years, you may not have another significant leap to make. But the same process that leads to a leap will help stave off age-related decline as long as possible.

We can imagine an athlete's career in the next chart. An athlete can make many leaps, and each will have the same stages: Build, Leap, Sustain. *The difference between making a leap and not making a leap is in the quality of our training.*

"The difference between making a leap and not making a leap is in the quality of our training."

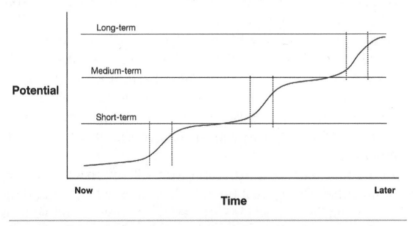

Fig 9 · Reaching our long-term potential requires us to continually create new leap cycles

Every leap is preceded by a change. The most effective changes are improvements in quality–how well we train–which compound over time. For most of us, improving our mental approach to training is the most effective change we can make. It's the change that's most likely to result in a major leap.

22

After you make a leap and enter the Sustain phase you need to figure out where you can again increase the quality of your training. This could mean doing higher quality workouts, doing the same workouts even better, doing more while maintaining your quality, or improving areas of your life that indirectly affect your training.

No matter how big a leap you make in the short-term, it won't get you to your long-term potential. You simply can't reach your potential in a few months. It will take multiple leaps over multiple years.

But I have good news: the first leap is the easiest! It doesn't really take that much.

"The good news: the first leap is the easiest!"

Your first leap should come within one season to one year. It depends in part on where you are and on how positive your feedback loop becomes.

If you can continually improve your positive feedback loop, you will see further leaps in the mid-term (2-3 years), with long periods of build-up in between. These periods with zero visible improvement are normal, too. They are the times when your body is creating a new baseline. It's from these new baselines that you need to improve your quality so that it can grow into another leap.

In the long-term (7 to 10 years), you will approach achieving your potential. During that time, build phases get longer and the leaps get smaller—you can't keep taking one minute off your 5k time forever—but they are still there. And throughout, your "normal" will become consistently excellent.

As coaches, this is what we want from all our runners. And it is completely natural, predictable, and achievable. But only if our training and our lifestyles are creating the positive feedback loop to make it happen. Our lifestyles determine our leap cycles.

Key Takeaways

1. Anyone can make a leap in their performance. A leap is the natural output of maintaining a positive feedback loop in your training.

2. Improvement appears linear in the beginning but is actually exponential. Consistent, high quality training leads to making a leap.

3. A "leap cycle" has three main stages—Build, Leap, and Sustain—and can be repeated indefinitely until you reach your potential.

4. All leaps are preceded by a change in training quality. If your quality doesn't improve after making a leap, you will not make another one.

Spotlight: The Momentum Model

I will use these "spotlights" to introduce some mental models or theories that help to make the concepts stick. The first mental model I want to introduce is one I've been developing for many years. I call it the "Momentum Model."

The Momentum Model

Imagine you are a ball. You are on an uphill path with a goal at the end. The height of the goal is the amount you have to improve to achieve it. The length of the path is how long it will take to get there.

To reach your goal, you need to pick up enough momentum (i.e. improve) to ascend the hill and overcome any potential obstacles on the path.

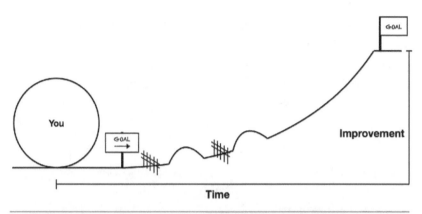

Fig 10 · To achieve a goal, you need to generate sufficient momentum to climb the hill and overcome the obstacles in the way.

Where your ball sits represents your current ability. From your current position, there are three possibilities: go forward, go backward, or stay where you are.

Now imagine that there are positive forces that make you roll faster, and negative forces that slow you down. Simple, right? The more the positive forces outweigh the negative, the faster you will roll toward your goal. This is conceptually the same idea as having a positive feedback loop.

These positive and negative forces exist within you or outside you. We can represent them with arrows. The arrows pointing toward your goal are positive and those pointing away are negative.

> *"The only way to reach your goal is to get more or stronger arrows pointing in the right direction."*

The only way to reach your goal is to get more or stronger arrows pointing in the right direction. You can achieve this by increasing the positive forces in your life, or by decreasing the negative forces. Or ideally, both.

Positive & Negative Forces: The Drivers of Momentum

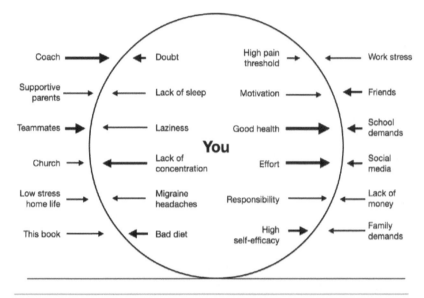

Fig 11 - The forces that move our ball can be positive or negative and internal or external.

We don't just automatically make progress toward our goals. Forces have to align to move us in the right direction. These forces can be internal or external, and positive or negative.

Internal forces fall into three general categories: our health, our attitudes, and our efforts. Some of these we control, others less so. The image above shows many examples of internal forces (there are many more than can fit in this picture).

External forces include the people and organizations in our lives, as well as our general environment. Some of these push us forward and help us achieve our goals. Others hold us back. Some affect us personally, while others–like the coronavirus–affect everyone.

It is up to us to identify our internal and external forces and either eliminate the negative forces or boost the positive ones.

Five Insights About the Forces

1. The size of the arrow indicates its strength. Not all arrows are equally strong. Big arrows push us harder than small ones.

2. The size of an arrow changes over time. Arrows get bigger or smaller. We can strategically increase or decrease their strength over time.

3. The direction of the arrows are not fixed. A positive force today can turn negative tomorrow. It is up to us to keep our forces positive.

4. We can't perfectly measure all the arrows affecting us. The best we can do is make a rough guess. It's sufficient to stick with the following two questions:
- Is this a positive force or a negative force?
- Is it as strong or as weak as I want it to be?

5. Talent is best understood as the size of your ball. Talent is not an internal force. It is us. A talented person can gain more ground with each push. But that doesn't stop someone with less talent from pushing harder and achieving more.

Obstacles and our Chosen Path

Most of us choose a goal, and then decide a path to get there. How high that goal is and how much time we have will both affect how much momentum we need to generate.

Big leaps are possible in a short time. But there is only so much momentum you can sustain. It's not possible to generate enough momentum to achieve your long-term potential in one giant leap.

It's useful to take another look at the Leap Cycle chart. Long-term goals are achieved by making successive leaps. We gain momentum (Build), move up the hill (Leap), and then crest for a while (Sustain) until we regain more momentum.

"Long-term goals are achieved by making successive leaps."

While the idea of making an uber-Leap–shown in the dashed line below–is enticing, it isn't possible.[14] We can roll a ball up a small hill. We can't roll a ball up the side of a cliff.

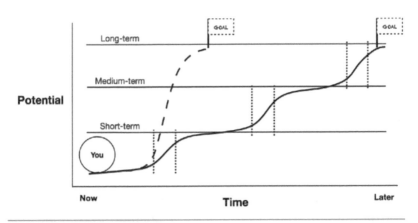

Fig 12 · The "Uber-leap" shown in the dashed line is not possible; it takes multiple leaps to achieve our potential

But there's one more thing we need to factor in: obstacles.

Persistence obstacles are things we can overcome only by digging in and pushing through them. Running 100 mile weeks, training through rough winters, etc.

Preparation obstacles are events that we can anticipate and strategize for. Final exam week. A difficult work schedule. Challenging weather.

Bad luck obstacles are events we can't really prepare for. A relative dies, a thief steals your bag, dropping a table on your toe, etc.

---

[14] I do not consider Jon Rankin's leap to qualify. Despite the fact he did not run much faster in his career, I do believe he had the potential to make more improvements had health issues not cut short his career.

Obstacles rarely stop our progress, but they often slow us down. The best way to overcome an obstacle is to anticipate it and avoid it. If that's not possible, it is best to have a system in place to maintain as much positive momentum as possible when you hit them. Obstacles seem insurmountable when nothing else is going well, when we have no momentum.

The flip side is when you expect something to be an obstacle but you blow right past it. That's when you know you're on a roll.

Momentum = Positive Feedback Loops

The Momentum Model is a tool. It gives us a clean way to think about creating a positive feedback loop. Positive feedback loops are important to understand conceptually, but hard to apply in practice. Momentum is easy to understand, and the the idea of positive and negative forces is intuitive.

Use the Momentum Model to help make the ideas we discuss more concrete.

PART I: Attitudes, Beliefs and Values

Chapter 2: The Optimal Training Pyramid
- *Optimal Training Principle (OTP) #1: Your athletic performance is a result of your attitude, your effort, and your training methods*
- Attitude: The Foundation of Training
- Effort: Quality vs Quantity vs Time
- Training Methods: Refining Your Raw Materials

Chapter 3: Engagement
- *OTP #2: Active engagement in training makes the process more understandable, more relevant, and more effective. (And more fun.)*
- Curiosity and Understanding
- Perspective and Relevance
- Understanding the "Hidden Training Program"
- Engagement and Enjoyment
- Engaging the Disengaged

Chapter 4: Responsibility
- *OTP #3: You are responsible for your own training.*
- The Classic Division of Responsibility
- The Optimal Division of Responsibility
- The Role of Your Coach
- Responsibility for the Results

2. The Optimal Training Pyramid: Laying the Right Foundation

ere's a little secret between you and me.[15]
Here's the core of every training program of every elite runner ever: Run. A lot. Usually hard, occasionally easy.

That's an oversimplification, but it's still true. Training is only as complicated as we choose to make it. The same goes for our mental approach. We don't need to over-complicate it.

A compass is just a needle pointing north. But knowing how to use it can keep you going in the right direction. Your mental approach is the compass for your training.

It's time to dive into what I call the Optimal Training Principles. They are the foundation for how great athletes think about

---

[15] Good. You found me. I put the secret here so that only the smart people will find it.
Here it is: Running is a very simple sport.
(Don't tell anyone.)

training.[16] Each principle highlights a fundamental truth about training.

Just like the compass, adopting these Optimal Training Principles will keep you pointed in the right direction. Getting where you need to go is up to you.

Optimal Training Principle (OTP) #1: Your athletic performance is a result of your attitude, your effort, and your training methods

Fig 13 - The Optimal Training Pyramid - Attitude is the foundation. Effort is based on it, and Training Methods refine it.

The Optimal Training Pyramid above consists of three parts: attitude, effort and training methods. *Attitude* forms the foundation of an individual's success. Our *effort* is supported by and depends on our attitude. Our *training methods* sharpen that effort into its final shape.

> *"Attitude forms the foundation of a person's success."*

---

[16] From here on out, every elite athlete interview will read like a collection of quotes describing these principles.

Your Attitude is the Foundation of Your Training

Attitude is the foundation of Optimal Training. There are hundreds of beliefs and thoughts and ideas that contribute to our success, but I want to highlight the most important here. We'll really dig into these later.

Attributing Performance to Effort: We all think differently to some extent—we have different personalities, dream different dreams, set different limits, and enjoy different things—but there are a few attitudes all excellent performers share. A belief in the power of hard work is the most important.

Elite athletes get where they are by working smarter, harder, and longer than everyone else. They know success isn't solely due to effort, but they embrace effort because *it is the one factor they can control.*

I bet you already have this attitude with regard to running. But do you believe this about your grades, work and relationships as well?

Engagement: Motivation and passion seem similar but are actually quite different. Motivation is the desire to achieve a goal. Passion is an intense interest, regardless of a specific outcome. Both motivation and passion can drive you to invest your energy in an activity:

- You can be motivated to get a grade, but passion is what makes you excited to talk about what you're learning
- You can get motivated to write a report, but passion is what keeps you up at night writing a blog
- And (at least in my case) I know I could get motivated enough to complete a triathlon, but I'm only passionate about running

Optimal Training requires that we be both motivated and passionate. When we put both together and apply them, we get engagement.

Why is engagement so important? Because it keeps us experimenting, asking questions, challenging our assumptions, and learning. The level of our engagement directly affects the quality and quantity of our effort.

Responsibility: There is a big difference between being a fan and being an athlete. A fan can enjoy the outcome without feeling any responsibility; they make no decisions and hold no accountability. An athlete does not have that luxury. They must make decisions, often under incredible stress and time constraints, and they must hold themselves accountable for their decisions and actions.

It begins with the choices we make. Some can (and should) be delegated, primarily to our coaches. Once a decision is made, we need to be held accountable for how we execute it. If we make a bad decision, we need to get that feedback and we need to learn from it. If we make a good decision but execute it poorly, we need to hold ourselves accountable for that, too.

Taking responsibility means holding yourself accountable for what you can control: the choices you make and how you execute them.

Discipline: Another attitude shared by the best of the best is the ability to focus on what is important and de-emphasize what isn't. Note the word de-emphasize. It's an illusion that elite athletes are always disciplined. They are simply prioritizing and de-emphasizing, and have built routines into their lives to make it easier for them.

Discipline is the end product of focus and effective systems. Focus applies primarily to our workouts, where we strive to always do what we need to do *right now* to be our best *at some time in the future*. It requires that we practice purposefully, and restrain ourselves from doing too much. This is the case for today's workout, this weekend's race, and this year's training program.

Outside of practice it means engaging in momentum-positive behaviors and conserving as much energy as possible. It means having effective systems to keep you going forward without wasting your mental willpower.

How do you do this? You have to be engaged enough in your training to figure it out.[17]

Pride: Last but not least athletes need to have pride, which I think of as a combination of competitiveness and integrity. Most great athletes display a mix of wanting to be their best and push themselves to their limits, while wanting to beat the pants off anyone else when they compete.

But if you don't have integrity, any success you achieve will be hollow. Integrity is what separates those willing to cheat from those who pursue success honestly. True champions don't let winning become the only measure of their success. Their focus is as much on their execution and development as their outcome relative to the competition.

You must take pride in your performances. Pride shouldn't come from winning. It *should* come from *how you prepare and perform*. Even when the final result isn't what you wanted, you can still be proud of your performance.

Attributing Performance to Effort, Engagement, Responsibility, Discipline, and Pride. It starts here. If all of these are strong arrows pointing in the right direction, you're already well on your way to achieving your goals.

Effort: Quality, Quantity and Time

The simplest way to analyze effort is to break it down into its three main components: *quality, quantity, and time*. You can do something better, do more of it, or do it longer.

To start, focus on quality. Why? Because it gets harder and harder to maintain quality the more you increase quantity.

Quality tends to refer to two different things:
- Efficiency - how well you do something, and

---

[17] And keep reading. We'll cover this in detail as we go.

- Effectiveness - how appropriate an activity is

When we discuss effort, we are talking about efficiency. We'll discuss effectiveness when we get to Training Methods.

If you can get the same results using less time and energy, then that's what you should be doing. A perfectly efficient workout, for example, would have no wasted time or energy at all. You would arrive, warm up, kick butt, cool down, and go home expending just enough energy and no more.

The chart below shows **the Attitude-Effort Curve.** There is a direct connection between how you think about your training and the quality of your effort. As your attitudes improve, so does the quality of your effort. As your mental approach becomes consistently great, your workouts will become consistently high quality. Champions live in this range.

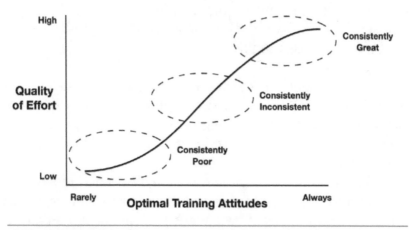

Fig 14 · The Attitude-Effort Curve. The more consistently your attitude is great, the higher quality your effort will be.

Right now, no matter how good you are, you need to ask yourself: can you train better? Once you accept that you can, it's just a matter of figuring out how.

Start by asking a simple question: *what is the purpose of this activity?*

"Start by asking a simple question: what is the purpose of this activity?"

Quality does not mean intensity, complexity, or bursts of activity. *Quality is determined by the workout's purpose.* I first learned this from a conversation with my coach, Bob Larsen.

As a redshirt freshman at UCLA, I didn't understand the purpose of my road runs. I just considered them easy days between interval workouts. I believed intervals were the workouts that made you fast.

I went into Coach Larsen's office to ask about the next interval workout. He instead asked me how my road runs were going. He asked how hard I was running them ("Pretty easy") and why ("Because intervals"). He stared at me for a moment and then he asked me why we do the road runs. He leaned back in his chair with a piercing stare and a bemused grin.

I felt trapped. He was the bobcat, and I was his prey.

("Umm...because running?")

He pounced.

He argued I put too much emphasis on intervals. We train seven days a week but we only do intervals twice. I had it all backwards. The secret to getting better is in the road runs. The quality of our road runs determines our general ability. Intervals simply refine it.

I didn't need to optimize my intervals. I needed to stop jogging and start training. My new goal should be seven high quality workouts, even if it meant I got a little less out of the interval sessions.

I took his advice. I ran my road runs increasingly harder. And over the course of that year I got steadily stronger, built some momentum, and even scored a couple surprise points at the PAC-10 Championships. Most importantly, I did it while avoiding another injury.

"Quality is determined by the workout's purpose."

Quality is a measure of execution. And execution is about how well your actions align with your purpose.

If we need a recovery day, the highest quality workout *is to take it easy.* Getting extra sleep could be much more important than getting in an extra interval or a few more miles. Seven high quality workouts per week doesn't mean seven hard workouts. It means seven well-executed workouts.

When you are executing everyday. When each workout is high quality. When your feedback loop is a well-oiled machine you're all set to make a leap.

Don't get impatient at this point. Remember, it's ok if you don't see improvement right away. The improvement will happen quickly when it does, but it takes some time to build to it.

If you want to speed up the process, to super-charge your feedback loop, there's a right way and a wrong way.

The right way is to improve the non-workout aspects of your life. Get more sleep. Eat better. Stretch more. Study more about the sport. Do activities that help you retain a little more of each day's progress.

The wrong way is to immediately increase **quantity**. Runners without an Optimal Training mindset often equate improvement with "doing more." That's because they see themselves on a linear improvement path, and the only way to improve faster is to do more. But this thinking leads to overtraining, increased injury risk, and a lot of wasted time and energy.

Thoughtlessly doing more is a lazy person's path to improvement. You think you're working harder, but you're just *making it harder*...on yourself.

Here's a simple rule of thumb. 70% quantity at 100% quality is better than 100% quantity at 70% quality.[18]

---

[18] Don't stress the 70%. It's directionally correct, and using an actual number makes it easier to remember. If your only disagreement is with the number, then you've already accepted the premise.

It's much harder to maintain high quality as your mileage increases. Low quality leads to fatigue, injury and poor execution. These are all negative inputs into your feedback loop. They are momentum killers. Keep them out of there!

Remember, you don't need to increase quantity to make a big leap. The two major components of a leap are quality (the positive feedback loop) and **time**. If you have the patience and discipline to maximize your quality over a sustained period of time, you're doing enough to make a leap.

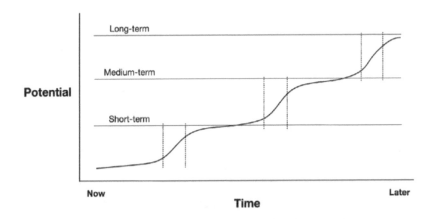

Once you've made a leap, you will find yourself back in a Sustain/Build phase. This is the time to consider increasing quantity. Not before, but after the leap.

But this is critical: *never increase quantity at the expense of quality.* If you can do more and maintain your quality, then it can lead to another leap. If doing more reduces your quality, if it weakens your positive feedback loop, then you're actually hurting yourself.

"Never increase quantity at the expense of quality."

Increasing quantity is a key part of every elite runner's training. But mileage is not an indicator of effort. Quality must come first.

Consult with your coach, your mentors, or other resources to determine what mileage you need to be running. If you eventually want to be at 130 miles per week but you are currently at 50... don't rush it. Do the best 50 you can, increase quantity only when you are ready, and remember that time is on your side.

Training Methods: Refining your Raw Materials

"There are many paths to the top of Mt. Fuji."
- Japanese proverb

If our attitude, effort and talent are our "raw materials," our training methods are how we polish them into a finished product.

I use the words "training methods" to mean *any activity that has an effect on your ability.* This can be both formal and informal.

In running, formal training activities include your workouts, weight training, stretching, icing, eating, hydrating, sleeping, keeping a training log, visualizing, etc. Anything we do with a specific aim to improve.

Informal activities might include neutral activities like studying, working, dating or pursuing other hobbies, but also any other behavior that might affect our training: smoking, binging (food, drink, Netflix), partying, roughhousing, playing pick-up basketball, etc.

You probably find it strange to include these informal activities as part of our "training methods." But they matter. A lot. Each of these activities contributes to our overall performance, albeit some to a greater degree than others. These informal activities make up part of the Hidden Training Program.

We talked about efficiency—how well we use our effort—as a measure of quality. The second measure of quality is "effectiveness." Effectiveness is a measure of how much value we can expect from an activity given the same amount of effort.

Effectiveness is the most straightforward way to measure training methods.

Weight training, for example, will never have as much impact on a runner's performance as the running workouts they do. Given the choice to do only one, running is the more effective activity.

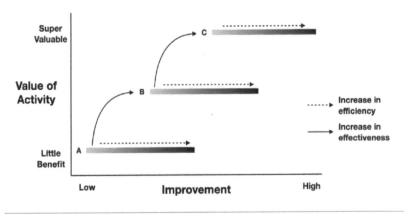

Fig 15 - Efficiency vs Effectiveness. Effectiveness is a measure of value, or how much an activity is worth. Efficiency is how well you do it, or how much energy is spent doing it.

But each can be viewed independently on an "effectiveness scale," ranging from "provides little benefit" to "super valuable." In the chart above, running may be a level C activity and weight training may be a level B. Its baseline value isn't as high, but if you lift the right way, it can help you improve.

Now I'm going to hit you with a "hot take." There are only two groups of runners who need to worry about effectiveness in their formal training programs.

1. Beginners (high school, first year, inexperienced coach), who just need to get a solid plan in place, and
2. Elites, who must optimize every workout and will be hurt by a sub-optimal training program

For the rest of us, if we have an experienced coach, we are probably getting decent guidance. If you aren't coached you can get on the internet and get good advice on workouts or training programs. The differences between specific workouts is minimal.

Put your energy into improving your mental approach, your preparation, and your effort.

I opened with a Japanese proverb: "There are many paths to the top of Mt. Fuji." That is true. But I've climbed Mt. Fuji and there's something that proverb leaves out: 99% of people use the same path!

Why? Because it's the simplest, most straight-forward, proven way to the top.

You don't need to blaze your own trail, inventing new and innovative workouts to try and get ahead of the competition. You just need a well-structured plan that you can execute purposefully and consistently. Trust me, most people don't execute purposefully or consistently. But the best do.

So here's another rule of thumb[19]: It's better to get 100% out of a good workout than 70% out of a perfect one.[20]

Why? Because high quality work generates more momentum. It leaves runners feeling more confident, more prepared, and more energized than low quality work. It leads to better engagement, more responsibility, and greater discipline. *Quality begets more quality.*

And because I can sense that hint of doubt you are feeling, let me ask just one question: who is more likely to identify a problem in the training program, a runner putting in 100% quality effort or a runner putting in 70% quality effort?

You already know the answer, but I'll say it anyway. Unless you are putting in 100% quality effort, *you will never know if the problem is the training program or you.*

---

19 This will be the last one. Two rules for two thumbs.

20 For those of you who prefer it spelled out in efficiency/effectiveness terms: A 70% effective workout executed 100% efficiently is preferable to a 100% effective workout executed 70% efficiently.

"Unless you put in 100% quality effort, you will never know if the problem is the training program or you."

Training methods are obviously an important aspect of a training program. But they are like the interior design in a house. It doesn't matter how stylish the house is if it isn't built on a solid foundation with quality materials. It will just be the illusion of a good house.

Similarly, an athlete following a perfect training plan with a bad attitude and low quality effort won't be more than the illusion of a well-trained athlete.

Key Takeaways

1. Your attitude, effort, and training methods are the three driving forces for all performances. Of these, attitude is the most important, because it determines the quality of the other two.

2. Quality, quantity and time are all critical aspects of our training. For most athletes, quality and time are sufficient to make their first leap.

3. Your focus should be on maximum efficiency, because it creates positive feedback loops and helps to identify opportunities to improve your training effectiveness.

3. Engagement: The Catalyst of Success

There is one essential quality I look for in a potential training partner, colleague, or friend: engagement. If someone is engaged, I know we have the potential to succeed. If not, success is unlikely.

An engaged person finds the root of the problem, considers all the likely possibilities, and works hard to achieve a positive outcome. Contrast this with their counterpart–the disengaged person–who can't be bothered and doesn't know enough to make a difference, who coasts on their natural talent and rides on the coattails of others.

Everything is made better through engagement. Intelligence plus engagement leads to breakthroughs. Caring plus engagement leads to improvement. Curiosity plus engagement leads to learning. So let's talk about engagement.

OTP #2: Active engagement in training makes the process more understandable, more relevant, and more effective. (And more fun.)

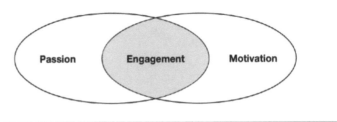

Fig 16 · Engagement is the result of passion meeting motivation.

My back of the envelope definition of engagement is "what happens when passion meets motivation." When you love what you do, and you are determined to achieve a goal, you will fully engage in your training.

> *"Engagement is what happens when passion meets motivation."*

Passion is an essential component of sustained success. If you aren't passionate about what you are doing, it's hard to sustain the level of effort you need to be great. (It's hard even if you are passionate.) But passion isn't just about doing the work; it's about being immersed in it, consumed by it, "getting it."

If you are passionate you want to learn more, talk about your training, and be around others who share your passion.

Motivation is about action. It pushes you forward to improve, to learn, to achieve. Whereas passion is about some *thing*, motivation is about *us*.

You can be passionate about running–reading books, buying lots of accessories, and jogging everyday–but not motivated to achieve a goal. You can also be motivated to win a race without being passionate about training. In either case, you may have some measure of success. But to sustain success–to truly be excellent–you need both.

Curiosity drives understanding

One sign of an engaged athlete is an intense curiosity in their training. They want to know everything. Why am I doing these workouts? What are other people doing? How does this fit in the bigger picture? Engaged athletes ask good questions.

Curiosity can take other forms. Reading books and blogs, watching documentaries, following successful athletes on social media, working or volunteering to learn more about something, and connecting what you learn in other areas of life to your training.

Curious runners are open to trying new workouts, experimenting, and analyzing their own performance. The more they do, the more they come to understand themselves, their strengths and weaknesses, and their areas for improvement.

One of the best ways to stay engaged is to investigate when your results don't align with your expectations. I had an experience at a meet that piqued my curiosity and ultimately changed how I warmed up before races. At the time, my warm-up was to start jogging about 50-60 minutes before the race, stretch leisurely, do 8-10 strides, and be ready to start.

At this meet there was an unexpected delay in the start time. We had all done our normal warm-ups but were told we had to wait for them to fix a technical problem. We all hung around the starting line doing strides and stretching. I must have done 20 extra strides during the delay.

I expected the extended warm-up to reduce my energy but it did exactly the opposite. I'd never felt so good at the start!

For perhaps the first time I my life, I was curious about warming up. I asked Coach Larsen if he thought it was possible to warm up too much. He didn't think that was anything to be concerned about. I decided to add 20 minutes or so to my warm-up routine and felt noticeably better at the start of races.

Curious athletes will question why they do things and whether there is a better way. They will try to identify the (often unspoken) assumptions driving their beliefs. I had never truly questioned my warm-up routine and how to improve it. It took that experience to spark my curiosity. But once I acted on it, I found an easy opportunity for improvement.

Here are a few ideas that should engage your curiosity:

- Read one or two books about training, not to change your program but to understand the science or history of each type of workout. I valued my long runs much more after reading a book about marathon training, even though at the time I wasn't planning to run a marathon.
- Do thought experiments. Ask yourself (or others) what would happen if...? Playing out these scenarios can often lead to ideas that spark your curiosity, especially if you are discussing with someone thoughtful.
- Study the history of world record progression for a few events. Look for major improvements and then read about the people who made those leaps. What did they do differently? Watch their races on YouTube where they are available.
- Check out one or two running websites to keep track of the latest news. Pick a current pro, if possible somebody in your event, and make a point to read all the articles and watch all the videos about that person.
- Get in pointless debates with your teammates on long runs and easy days. Ranking historical athletes or favorite courses can be a fun way to pass the time while still learning something.[21]

Perspective drives relevance

---

[21] Or you can debate things like, "which animal would win in a fight, a hippo or a grizzly?" This random question spawned such a debate that it still comes up when we get together!

The big benefit that comes from understanding your training is a sense of perspective. And this perspective makes your future decisions more relevant.

Understanding your training doesn't guarantee you will get the outcome you want. It just helps you make good decisions. Or at least make your decisions for the right reasons.

It may be the first time *you* are having an experience, but I assure you countless people have had it before you. There is little you can do that hasn't already been done by someone else. If not exactly, then close enough to learn from. And if you can learn from how they handled it, you can apply that to your own benefit.

The first time I developed a stress fracture, I ended up training in the pool for many weeks. I'd never done it before and didn't even know what it meant to "run in the pool" the first day I went there.[22] But my teammate Scott was also in the pool that day and explained the basics, including telling me some of the things he'd done in the past to have a good workout. It really helped.

Having a well-rounded perspective also allows you to practice more purposefully and to manage expectations throughout the season. It allows you to maintain your equilibrium when things aren't going as expected. And it gives you the opportunity to find your unique place, the place where you provide the most value and get the most enjoyment.

The following will help you ensure your training is relevant:

- Keep a training diary and look for ways in which your training is changing over time. If these changes don't make sense (curiosity alert!) ask your coach about them.
- Talk to your coach about your stages of training (base building, strength training, speed training, tapering, recovery) and the workouts that will go into them.

---

[22] It turns out "running in the pool" means "running in the pool." You go in the deep end, and then run back and forth trying not to drown.

- Read about other athletes' training cycles, and compare them to the work you are doing (not the times, but the types of workouts).
- Try to learn about what great athletes did prior to making their leaps. Leaps are usually preceded by lifestyle changes. Consider whether those changes make sense for you, too.

Understanding the Hidden Training Program[23] drives effectiveness

You may not have realized this, but there are in fact two training programs that every athlete must carry out. The first is their official, formal, coach-approved training program. This is what is expected of you as a member of the team.

The second is the Hidden Training Program: everything you *really* need to do to be successful.

> *"The Hidden Training Program is everything you **really** need to do to be successful."*

The Hidden Training Program includes the formal training program and much more. How you prepare before practice and recover afterward. How you eat and drink to maximize your energy. How you allocate your time to other responsibilities (school, work, family, partner). How you talk to your coaches to have productive conversations.

Success is about more than just showing up and working hard. You have to be ready to work hard when you show up!

Olympic 800 meter runner Khadevis Robinson told me a story once about how he approached eating when he was traveling in Europe. He would bring his own oatmeal and peanut butter from the US. He knew he could get oatmeal or peanut butter in Eu-

---

[23] I modified this idea from the concept of the Hidden Curriculum, first published by Philip W. Jackson in his book *Life in Classrooms*

rope, but he wanted everything about his experience to be as predictable and consistent as possible.[24]

Have you given any thought to your oatmeal or peanut butter recently? The best athletes have.

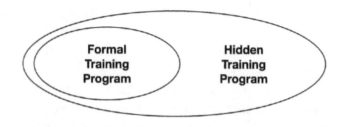

Fig 17 · The Hidden Training Program is everything you REALLY need to do to be successful. The Formal Training Program makes up just a part of it.

Whereas your formal training program is communicated directly, the Hidden Training Program is rarely communicated at all. It is learned through engagement: watching how others behave, seeing how people react to different situations, listening to how people talk, and identifying the routines that separate the best from the rest.

My uncle told me a story about his time running at Cal Poly San Luis Obispo in the early 1980s. They had a very strong team, and he was looking to improve so he could make the traveling squad.

He decided to go to the library to check out books on running and see if he could gain some insight or advantage. He checked out every book he could find. When he got home and looked at the little card indicating who had checked the books out before him, all the top runners on his team had already read the books!

Great runners are always fully engaged in their training. You will have to match their engagement to compete with them.

The Hidden Training Program also consists of all the unstated expectations of those around us. Not everyone on your team is

---

[24] KD was a guest on the Go Be More Podcast on 6/19/2020.

making you better. They may not even realize it. But the expectations they set for you can help you or hinder you.

The best teams reinforce optimal training habits in every aspect of their day. In doing so, they reveal the Hidden Training Program more directly to new teammates, who quickly see that there is a specific way they will need to behave in order to succeed. This is the best case scenario, but unfortunately not every team has created an environment of excellence for new members to step into.

When I arrived at UCLA, I had no idea what I was doing.[25] So I did what we all do in these situations: I copied what others did. But outside of practices, everybody did different things. At one end, Meb was insanely thorough and disciplined. We would joke that he wouldn't spit without first considering whether it affected his training.

Then there was the rest of the team. Most guys drank and partied. Some did ultrasound treatments and massages before workouts, but others didn't. After practice some guys did ice baths, some wrapped ice on sore muscles, and some skipped icing altogether. Some stretched well and others hardly at all. Some ate amazing amounts of food and others tried to eat healthy. Some guys did core work after practice and others did it at home or not at all. One or two pledged fraternities, a couple others had jobs, and a few others volunteered.

It was up to us as individuals to know what we needed and use the resources available. But I didn't know what I needed. I'd never thought about any of this stuff before.

I sort of fell into the routine of the "other guys," the non-elite members of the team. I followed their leads, but inconsistently. I stretched, but not purposefully. I iced, but only when it felt necessary. I did some sit-ups, sometimes, when I thought about it. I rarely asked the trainers for treatment because I felt embarrassed about it...surely better athletes needed their attention more.

---

[25] See also: the shoelaces story in the introduction.

I can see now that Meb understood–either explicitly or implicitly–the Hidden Training Program, and structured his entire life around it. Other guys either understood it but didn't care as much, or (and I think this is more likely) didn't understand it at all.

The formal training program and the resources available to athletes at UCLA was world-class. But the Hidden Training Program required athletes to be fully engaged, know what they needed, and take responsibility to get it. Some guys thrived. Others, like me, took more time to figure it out.

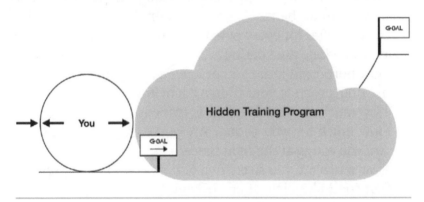

Fig 18 - The Hidden Training Program is everything you REALLY need to do to be successful.

You can picture the Hidden Training Program as a kind of fog that obscures the negative forces and obstacles on the path to your goal. The more you expose it, the clearer the path to success will be. The more you allow it to stay hidden, the more likely you or your teammates will be slowed down by it.

When Coach Larsen retired, Eric Peterson and Helen Lehman-Winters took over. They made some significant changes. They formalized many activities from the Hidden Training Program. We all stretched together as a team. We all did core work as a team. We did weight training as a team. We were expected to get pre- and post-workout treatment.

By this point, I had started to figure this out on my own, but I appreciated the change. It gave the entire team a much clearer path to follow. It set higher and more consistent expectations.

And it created opportunities to reinforce optimal training behaviors.

Some of the concepts we've already discussed are part of the Hidden Training Program: positive feedback loops, how quality compounds and leads to leaps, identifying positive and negative forces, and acknowledging attitudes as the foundation of your training.

Your momentum and positive feedback loops are largely driven by the Hidden Training Program. In one sense, all we are doing together is exposing and explaining it.

If you want to be great, it's not enough to do hard workouts. You have to think better, figure out your Hidden Training Program (it will differ for every person and team), and train at a high quality over a long time period.

- How purposefully are you practicing? Do you know why you are doing each of your training activities?
- How much are you sleeping? Is that enough?
- How much are you eating? Are you eating the right foods? Are you eating at the right times?
- How much are you stretching or doing other "maintenance" activities, like icing, after workouts?
- Do you have non-training activities that are consuming too much of your time and energy? What can you do to find a better balance?

You can probably have some measure of success without worrying about all of these questions. But I can't stress this enough: your competition *will be thinking about every aspect of the Hidden Training Program. (Even the oatmeal.)* And if you **really** want to be successful, you need to as well.

*"I can't stress this enough: your competition **will be** thinking about every aspect of the Hidden Training Program. (Even the oatmeal.)"*

Engagement makes training more fun.

There is a fourth and additional benefit to engaging in your training. It makes it more fun!

Certain activities aren't inherently fun. The last few miles of a long run. Sitting in an ice bath after practice. Throwing up after an interval workout. But what happens once you've fully committed to doing them and no longer focus on the question, "Should I...?" You find ways to make them more bearable, maybe even enjoyable.

I have a little story about ice baths. In the training room at UCLA they have a few ice baths that they keep at 50 degrees (10° Celsius) for people to soak in after workouts. When I first arrived as a freshman, I had never iced in a meaningful way. Outside of my mom putting a pack of frozen peas on my head when I bonked it, icing was not something I did.

You should also know that I hate cold water. I'm skinny, I have no insulation, I have a condition called Raynaud's where my fingers and toes go white and numb in the cold, and within about 5 minutes I get a case of the shivers and want to get out. And I'm talking about swimming pools here. You can imagine how bad the ocean is. An ice bath? No way.

Most of the veterans soaked in the ice baths for 15 minutes after workouts. Meb was religious about it. He hopped in, opened a text book, and spent the 15 minutes reading. I...was not. I sometimes put my calves in, but the whole experience was miserable. I often just strapped ice packs to my calves and pretended I had someplace I needed to be. (I did. Anywhere but in an ice bath.)

One day our throws coach, Art Venegas, said that soaking in the ice bath reduces 70% of the tightness you experience the next day.[26] Crud. Now I had a choice. How bad did I want it?

I started getting in more consistently, and by talking to Meb and the other guys I developed a little system that helped me get

---

[26] Looking back on it, there's no way that number is correct. I have no idea what the real effect is. At the time his specificity seemed authoritative.

through it. First, I brought a small towel in with me, wrapped around my neck. For the first two minutes (which are by far the worst) I made a lot of faces, took deep breaths, squeezed the towel, and said ridiculous things like, "Hot side of Mercury. Surface of the sun." Try it. Even if it doesn't work, other people think it's funny.

Thinking hot thoughts, which I credit to my friend Andrew, wasn't actually something we did (well, I didn't). I just said it because it made me smile, and it eventually became a kind of joke mantra for us when we got in the bath. When somebody got in, another person would say it to them as a tiny bit of encouragement.

After a couple minutes, when my legs were beginning to get numb, I would either pull out a book to read or chat with people. Some days, that was enough. Other days I would start to get the shivers after about 5 minutes. On these days I would wrap the towel around my face and blow hot air into it. You'd be surprised how much it matters that your face is warm, even if the rest of your body isn't.

Is this the best way to get through an ice bath? I have no idea. I imagine Navy Seals have come up with better approaches. But it helped me get through it, and over time became a sort of enjoyable sub-routine within my overall training. I believe this contributed to my leap, because consistently icing was one of many positive changes I made to my training in the months prior. I turned a negative arrow (avoiding the ice bath) into two positives (better icing and team bonding).

Engagement in training keeps your positive arrows pointed in the right direction. It's fun to be on a roll. When you are really on a roll, obstacles don't feel like obstacles. They seem to just disappear.

Ask any hurdler: the hurdles are the same height no matter how fast you approach them, but going over them is a lot easier if you've got some momentum.

"Engagement in training keeps your positive arrows pointed in the right direction."

Engaging the disengaged

By now you are hopefully thinking about ways to get a little more engaged. Good! Me too, believe me. It's a constant struggle.

Sometimes, especially with young and inexperienced athletes, it's just about knowing how. I speak from experience, as I was embarrassingly disengaged when I was in high school.

I was immediately the fastest runner on my team, and the older athletes were equally inexperienced. I never picked up a book, paid attention to what anyone else was doing, or thought about how any other aspect of my life could affect my training.[27]

But I thought I was engaged. I was doing the workouts, enjoyed running, and cared about my results. I just didn't know what being truly engaged *meant*.

I attribute this now to three reasons: first, I was never exposed to anything like the Optimal Training mindset; second, none of my high school coaches or teammates were truly passionate about competitive running[28]; third, the Internet didn't (really) exist.[29]

Once I got to college, I was around teammates who knew a lot about the sport. I suddenly had access to high speed Internet (and discovered sites like LetsRun and Dyestat). And I was exposed to the kinds of classes and concepts that gave me the tools to re-evaluate my training.

Before I end this chapter, I want to relate a non-running story about the importance of engagement. I had the privilege to work

---

[27] Full disclosure: I didn't even know who Steve Prefontaine was until they made two documentaries about him, well after I'd been in college. Yeah.

[28] By this I don't mean knowledgeable about how to train. We did sophisticated workouts. We just didn't converse about great runners or their training.

[29] We had dial-up AOL. I'm old.

at Apple for many years, and I often get asked about what it's like to work there. In two words: brutally fulfilling.

It really could be brutal. It is a hierarchical company filled with micro-managers. Negative feedback is provided immediately and directly. People stress minor details as much as major issues. Expectations are extremely high. You are expected to anticipate the unpredictable (what Apple internally calls "seeing around corners") and to take accountability for things outside your control. Add to this long working hours and high stress. You can imagine why people wonder what I liked about the experience.

So here it is: working at Apple means working with people who are 100% engaged in their jobs. You cannot survive (let alone thrive) at Apple if you are not fully engaged. The result is every challenge you face is met with maximum creativity, perspective, effectiveness, motivation, and passion. When asked to give the one reason Apple is so successful, most analysts say things like "design," "marketing," "economies-of-scale." or "lock-in." They're wrong. The answer is "engagement."

Engagement is a skill. A learnable and transferrable skill that will not only improve your running, but set you up for success in whatever you do.

> *"Engagement is a learnable and transferable skill that will set you up for success in whatever you do."*

If you or a teammate are struggling to stay engaged, sometimes it just takes a little prompting. Pick up a biography of a former athlete, read the latest news about the sport, ask your coaches and teammates for ideas, talk about the ideas we are discussing now. Engagement is about channeling more effort into the activity, and it's perfectly fine to start small.

Key Takeaways

1. Engagement is a key Optimal Training attitude. By engaging you improve your understanding, your perspective, and your effectiveness.

2. The Hidden Training Program is everything you "really" need to do to be successful. Engagement is the best way to reveal the hidden training program.

3. Increasing engagement doesn't require huge efforts. It is sufficient to start small by reading, talking, and asking about your training.

4. Responsibility: Doing vs Delegating

When Lena Nilsson arrived at UCLA in the summer of 1999 she stood out from the typical freshman recruit. She had a discipline and professionalism that most of us lacked. She seemed destined to be great.

And she was. She won NCAA championships at 800m (indoors), 1500m (outdoors) and anchored the distance medley relay team to a sub-11 time and national title.[30]

Most of the runners at UCLA came from US high school programs, where coaches coached and runners ran. Choosing our college was often the first (and only) time we'd ever chosen a coach, and most of us were happy to be there. I was very much in this group.

Lena wasn't used to training that way, however. She came from Sweden, where she had been responsible for her own train-

---

[30] She defeated future Olympians Shalane Flanagan and Christin Wurth-Thomas to win those titles, and still holds the UCLA records for 800m and 1500m both indoors and outdoors.

ing for many years. She had left coaches and hired new ones to help her get to the next level. She'd chosen UCLA because it gave her the opportunities she was looking for, but she wasn't ready to hand Coach Peterson as much control as he expected to have.

This created some friction in the beginning.

Lena chafed at the idea of just doing what she was told. She wanted to understand what she was being asked to do. She wanted to play a role in every part of her training.

It took some time for both Lena and Coach Peterson to figure each other out. And when they did (and she was able to stay healthy) she was outstanding. But it wasn't the smoothest transition.

Lena's experience highlights a critical aspect of optimal training. Just as your coach's job is to get the best out of you, the reverse is also true. Your job is to get the most out of your coach.

OTP #3: You are responsible for your own training.

Taking full responsibility for your training is a critical component of maintaining your momentum. But it begs another important question: what about your coach?

What is the point in having a coach? Why bother? I mean, you are engaged. You know enough about yourself and how to train to draw up some good workouts. And you're mature enough to hold yourself accountable to your training. Why not just go it alone?

The Classic Division of Responsibility

If you haven't given this question serious thought, then chances are you haven't given enough thought to your training. If you've always had a coach and never thought twice about it, you may also recognize your own training in the chart on the next page.

Most athletes (myself included) start their training with this division of responsibility between themselves and their coach. The coach plans the workout (or the training schedule)

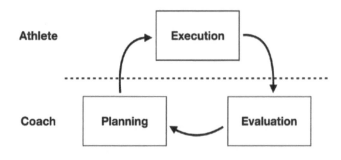

Fig 19 - The Classic Division of Responsibility: the coach plans and evaluates; the athlete focuses solely on execution

and you do what you are told. Your responsibility is to execute to your coach's specifications. After the workout (or race, or season) the coach evaluates your progress, and refines the next training program, which you then dutifully attempt to execute.

I'm not arguing this is always the case, or that there is no feedback happening in the process, or even that you never have a say in the evaluation or the planning. What I'm saying is that in this situation, the athlete *only takes responsibility* for one thing: executing the workout.

That's not optimal. It may be easy. It may be normal. It may be expected of you and what the coach wants. It may even be effective and efficient, particularly with inexperienced runners. But it is not optimal.

For you to realize your potential, **you must take responsibility for all aspects of your training**. You do not just have a coach, you *hire* a coach. You do not give up responsibility for planning and evaluation, but *delegate responsibility* to your coach. You do not run for your coach, but rather your coach *coaches for you.*

"For you to realize your potential, you must take responsibility for all aspects of your training."

The Optimal Division of Responsibility

The optimal division of responsibility for your formal training program looks more like this. I know, all I did was move the line! But that move makes a big difference.

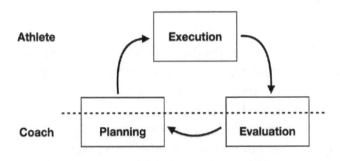

Fig 20 - The Optimal Division of Responsibility: the athletes shares some responsibility for planning and evaluation, too

Responsibility for Planning: You and your coach will share this responsibility. But it starts and ends with you.

You can delegate the main planning activities to your coach. In most cases this is the smart thing to do. They are experts after all. But when it comes time to "sign off" on the workouts, you have to give your input, express your reservations if you have any, and ensure that you agree with the plan.

Don't just accept trying to execute a plan you don't believe in. It rarely works. If your concerns are minor, remember what we discussed earlier: it's better to execute an average workout perfectly. If you have major concerns, it's your responsibility to work them out.

Responsibility for Execution: This is still all you.

To execute a workout or race effectively, you need to know what you are doing and why you are doing it. You also need to know the details, like how fast you should run or how much effort you should give. And then, you have to have the discipline to stick to that plan.

That means recovery runs are not run at road run pace and pace runs are not run all-out. Yes, you can fail to execute a workout by running too hard, too.

During the workout, you need to get feedback to help you improve. If you aren't getting it, ask for it. Don't just assume everything is optimal. Make sure.

Responsibility for Evaluation: Finally, when you are evaluating your performance, you cannot settle for being told how you are performing. Your input matters, too.

That doesn't mean you ignore your coach's opinions, or even that yours are more valid. It means you share ownership of the evaluation process and initiate it when necessary. You are responsible for not hiding things from your coach, for tracking your progress thoroughly (in a training log), and for not shying away from constructive criticism...because a good coach will give it to you!

If you can't take responsibility for these three roles, you are not ready to be your best. And having the best coach in the world isn't going to change that.

Responsibility for the Rest

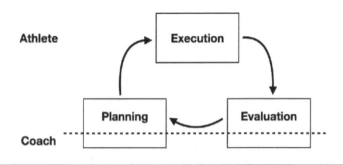

Fig 21 - Responsibility for the Hidden Training Program rests primarily with the athlete

So that covers the formal training program, the two to four hours of your day you spend with your coach. What about the Hidden Training Program, the other 20 hours? Good news. You own even more of the responsibility for this.

You are delegating a few hours a day to your coach. In these few hours you are doing tailored workouts with Next Step goals aimed at improving specific skills. Outside of these few hours, you are living your life. The decisions you make here can have just as big an impact on your momentum.

Your first leap, the one that is three to six months away right now as you read this, is almost certainly going to be the result of positive changes you make to your Hidden Training Program.

In the ideal state, you have everything under control. Your coach is available to provide guidance but isn't needed. That's not always going to be possible.

For younger or less mature runners, coaches may need to play a more active role in defining lifestyle guidelines for athletes. They don't need to be overly demanding, just useful systems that athletes can fall back on when making decisions.[31]

If you are ready to make these changes, let your coach know. Every coach wants to help their athletes make better choices and achieve better results. Use them, but don't rely on them to tell you what you need to do.

Ultimately, how you choose to spend your time outside of your workouts will be your decision, and you have to hold yourself accountable for it.

The role of your coach

Do you even need a coach?

Yes, you need a coach.

In fact, I'd go further and say you should have a coach for all areas of your life, not just training. A coach for your work, studies, hobbies, marriage... I believe the concept of a "coach" was

---

[31] Chapter 9 is dedicated to this topic.

one of the key innovations in history, yet somehow we've only formalized it in sports.

My challenge to you: have a coach, but reconsider the relationship. To quote my coach Bob Larsen: "Your job is to get the most out of your coach."[32] That's not a natural way for most athletes to think.

"Your job is to get the most out of your coach."

If you are in high school, you may not have a say in who coaches you. The coach is hired by the school and coaches whoever is on the team. They may or may not be hired for their expertise in coaching. But they are usually passionate, motivated people who enjoy developing young athletes. Figure out what their strengths are and try to supplement them with your own learning. If you aren't disrespectfully challenging their authority, most coaches will appreciate suggestions for improving your training.

University coaches are required to balance administrative expectations (signing top recruits, victories against rivals, conference championships, etc) with your expectations. What they need you to do can be different from what you want to do. Many runners quit or transfer because they did not consider this alignment when choosing the school. Take responsibility for this discussion and after you enroll, engage with your coach on these topics to keep your momentum as strong as possible.

Post-collegiate coaches are hired by you to develop you. They may have many other athletes they are coaching, but you should expect a one-to-one relationship with them. Many athletes choose to train in training groups and these can often be formed around the coach. Depending on who you want as a coach, you may need to move to live near them, not vice versa.

As you get older and more advanced in your training, you also get more choice in who coaches you and under what conditions.

---

32 From an interview on the Go Be More Podcast on 7/21/2020.

Regardless of the level, there are a fixed list of qualities most people look for:

- Experience and/or deep knowledge
- Passion for the sport and their athletes
- Expertise in creating training programs
- Strategic/Tactical skills (developing race plans, etc.)
- Motivational skills
- Administrative skills (i.e. organizing a trip to a track meet)
- Recruiting skills (if college, private high school or way too serious youth coach)
- Stopwatch management skills (3 at a time = bonus)
- Imitate-ability[33]

You will bring your specific strengths to the relationship. So will your coach. A coach who complements you and provides the qualities you need to excel is critical. It is your responsibility to choose the right person and/or make sure the relationship works.

Responsibility for the Results

After you've taken responsibility for your planning, execution, and evaluation, there's still one final step. That's taking **responsibility for the results**.

Lena Nilsson had a lot of success at UCLA. But her career ended much earlier than she expected. She suffered repeated stress fractures and despite trying to get healthy for years, she eventually retired.

Looking back on her career, she felt what she really needed was to be held back. Her problem wasn't doing the work, it was doing too much. Even when recovering from a stress fracture, she cross-trained so hard it never healed.

---

[33] This isn't a word, but shouldn't it be? Our ability to capture Coach Larsen or Coach Peterson with a simple wave or clap of the hands is something that still bonds my teammates and me together. This is a bonus quality.

She had trouble accepting this at the time. But now she says, it was clear. "Somebody needed to put a cast on me. I wasn't going to stop." Her drive to be the best was blinding her from doing what she needed to do. She sees that now.

"I made my own decisions. I made my own mistakes. There were plenty of things I could have done better. Ultimately, I was in control of the decisions," she tells me.

Sometimes the hardest part of taking responsibility is accepting a reality you don't want to believe.

> *"Sometimes the hardest part of taking responsibility is accepting a reality you don't want to believe."*

Responsibility for results means looking to yourself first when you don't perform as expected. It means assuming the problem lies with your effort and execution, not with the plan to be executed. It means caring that the planning, execution and analysis are all leading to positive outcomes.

It also means taking responsibility for your expectations. Happiness is a function of expectations. How many times have you been disappointed about a race but your coach felt everything went fine? That's a disconnect in your expectations, and an opportunity to engage more.

These tips will increase the responsibility you take for your results:

• Ask a lot of questions; don't settle for a vague understanding of what you are supposed to be doing; demand clarity

• Draft your own training program and compare it with your coach's; even when you go with your coach's training program, this will make you a more engaged runner and you will understand your training more completely

• Ask your coach to review your training log; compare what they see with what you saw on your own

- Manage your other responsibilities proactively; i.e. don't let homework keep you up all night when you need your rest for training, get it done early
- Choose your coach carefully; if you are going to college, don't just choose a successful program, choose a coach who you connect with
- Look to yourself first when things don't go right; you will fail, often, and when you do, evaluate your role in that failure before looking to blame others

One more story. I am including this because I want you to make a leap, but I also want you to know how doing so can mess with your head.

I made a leap my junior year, becoming one of the top runners in the conference. This leap was the result of many factors: lifestyle changes, a new coach, and consistently applying all of these concepts.

One of the changes to my training was the introduction of tempo runs on the track, usually between 5-7 miles at 5-minute mile pace or so. I loved these workouts because they matched my strengths: establishing a rhythm, feeling my pace, and maintaining my consistency. They also conditioned me for the 10k on the track, the event I was most focused on.

During my senior year—post-leap—we switched my tempo run to a modified fartlek run. I wasn't comfortable with the change. My coach explained his reasoning and I executed it to the best of my ability. But I wasn't racing as well and this was the most obvious change. I decided the lack of tempo runs were to blame.

I wasn't running that far off from my bests the previous year. I wasn't as consistent, but I was still performing better than I ever had previously. My expectations were much higher, though. I expected to keep leaping. Why change what worked before?

Knowing what I know now, this is how I would chart my progress starting from my sophomore year. Steady but seemingly linear improvements until my junior year, a leap my junior year, and then a flattening as I reached my near-term potential. A completely normal leap cycle.

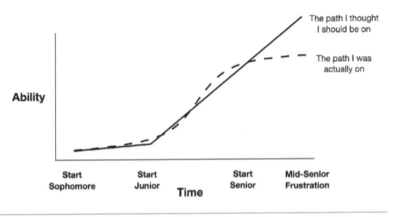

Fig 22 · Making a leap does not fit with linear expectations, and can cause frustrations when you come out of the Leap Phase and enter the Sustain Phase

That's not what I thought was happening, though. I thought improvement was linear and that my trajectory changed my junior year. Linear thinking can't explain a leap, and it messes with your expectations. When your performance starts to flatten out it feels like something is wrong, and you start looking for it. You find a reason that fits your mental framework. Mine was tempo runs.

> ## *"Linear thinking can't explain a leap, and it messes with your expectations."*

I can see now that in our conversations my coach was attempting to input a little more quality into my feedback loop. He was transitioning my leap cycle from Sustain to Build. At the time I didn't understand. Perhaps I was simply unwilling to.

Fartlek runs weren't the only change in my life at that time. I lived with different people and established different routines, my dad was ill and clearly depressed (he passed away that year), I had decided to move abroad with no plan to continue training, and I was reading a lot about topics that made me somewhat "anti-competitive." My attitude worsened, and it affected every aspect of my training. I disengaged, and little things started to slip.

But it was much easier to blame everything on the tempo runs. With every average performance, I looked at the training program as the problem. In the end, I had a frustrating senior year. Had you told me as a sophomore the times I would run that year I would have been ecstatic. But my expectations were higher, which made my frustration much worse.

Ultimately, the failure was mine. Not because my results were poor–they were close to my prior year performances–but because I didn't do what I needed to continue improving. I didn't take responsibility.

As you pursue your goals in running, take responsibility for your planning, execution, evaluation, and results. Start now. It's a necessary condition to being your best.

Key Takeaways

1. You are responsible for all aspects of your training, including planning, execution, and evaluation.

2. Your coach's role is to provide you the best possible guidance toward achieving your goals. You must engage with your coach to ensure you are getting the feedback you need.

3. Being responsible for the results means looking to yourself first when evaluating why you aren't performing to the level you aspire.

Spotlight: Attribution Theory

There is a difference between our results and the explanation we give for those results. No, the results *do not* "speak for themselves." We speak for our results, and high achievers do it better than low achievers.

What is Attribution Theory?[34]

Attribution is how we explain why things happen. For every event we create an explanation, a story we tell ourselves. Within those stories we attribute causes–correctly and incorrectly–to four factors:

---

[34] Technical footnote: Attribution theory started with the work of Fritz Heider in the early 20th century, but I am focused primarily on the research by Bernard Weiner, specifically on how students attributed their success and failure in academic settings.

Talent[35] is inherent to who we are. It's our *natural* ability (key word: natural).

Effort is how hard we work to achieve something. It includes our preparation, concentration, and execution.

Task difficulty is how hard we think it is to do something. This can relate to whether or not we'll succeed or to how much pain we will feel doing it.

Luck is what happens to us that we couldn't reasonably expect. Obviously this can be good or bad.

potential **Talent** genius natural strength knack inherent weakness endowed a head for... savant born to... gift aptitude comes easily incompetent capacity impotent the right stuff* savvy	train **Effort** procrastinate slack off idle try careless energy work hard give all we've got toil struggle prepare sluggish endeavor give our best shot lackadaisical push exercise put some elbow grease on it*
tough **Task Difficulty** challenging impossible difficult painful hellish hard crazy demanding basic a picnic complicated obvious a piece of cake simple smooth a snap straightforward easy as ABC* easy peasy lemon squeezy*	blessing **Luck** fate fluke destiny in the cards fortune karma serendipity a big/lucky break misfortune a raw deal a perfect storm cursed a tough/bad break untimely star-crossed jinxed schlemiel* schlimazel*

*grandparents only

Fig 23 - We use different words and phrases to attribute our success or failure to the four main factors

The chart above includes many of the common words we use when attributing performance. As you can see, we don't have to use the words, "It was a difficult task" to express that idea.

The stories we tell and the language we use to tell them is learned. We pick it up from our parents, friends, TV, movies, music, and other social interactions. The more you hear some-

---

[35] Weiner uses the word "ability" which I will later spend an entire chapter arguing is not the appropriate word for this context.

thing, the more likely you are to believe it. The more you believe it, the more likely you are to act on it.

Three Causal Dimensions

There is a second aspect of attribution theory we need to understand before we can tie it all together: the three causal dimensions of an attribution.

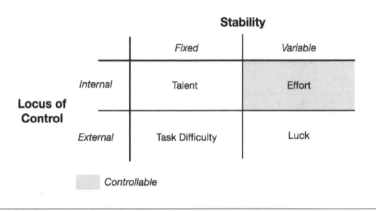

Fig 24 - Each factor can be categorized by Stability, Locus of Control, and Controllability

Locus of Control identifies whether the factor is internal (within us) or external (within the outside world). Internal factors are "Talent" and "Effort." External factors are "Task Difficulty" and "Luck."

Stability identifies whether the factor is variable or fixed. Speaking generally, "Talent" and "Task Difficulty" are fixed: they are what they are. "Effort" and "Luck" are variable: they can change at any time.

Controllability identifies whether we can control the factor or not, which means the factor must be both Internal and Variable. That leaves only "Effort." For attribution purposes, "Talent," "Task Difficulty," and "Luck"[36] are out of our control.

High Achievers vs Low Achievers

"High achievers and low achievers tell different stories."

High achievers and low achievers attribute their successes and failures to different factors. They tell different stories.

Attribution

		Success	Failure
	High Achiever	• Talented • Worked hard	• Didn't work hard • Underestimated task • Bad luck
Athlete			
	Low Achiever	• Task was easy • Lucky	• Not talented • Task too difficult

Fig 25 - High achievers internalize success and treat failure as variable. Low achievers do the opposite.

High achievers typically attribute success to internal factors: hard work, preparation, and natural talent. High achievers own their successes.

When high achievers fail, they don't attribute it to their talent. They attribute it to not working hard enough, to underestimating how hard the task would be, or when it's undeniable, to bad luck. For high achievers, nothing about failure is fixed.

Low achievers tend to attribute their success to either luck or the task being easy. They focus on external and uncontrollable factors. In doing so, they don't "own" their successes.

---

[36] No, you don't "make your own luck." That's called "Effort."

I used to tutor a boy in math. He showed me the results of his test and he had done much better than usual. He said, "I was so lucky the questions were the same as the ones we studied." So lucky!?!

He studied exactly what he needed to. He prepared correctly, did the work and earned the grade. But *he attributed his success to luck and not his own efforts*. And this next part is key. His attribution had no impact on the actual result. He still succeeded. He just didn't own it.

Finally, when low achievers fail they often attribute it to lack of talent or to the task being too difficult. I can't tell you how many times that same math student told me, "I just suck at math" or "Math is too hard for me." This is a devastating way to think because talent and task difficulty are fixed and uncontrollable. Why try when you've decided failure is inevitable?

Five Insights

1. High achievers internalize success. Low achievers externalize success. Success must be tied to you and your efforts. When it isn't, you can't own it.

2. High achievers view failure as variable. Low achievers view it as fixed. If failure is temporary, you can justify continuing. When it's fixed, the rational thing to do is move on.

3. High achievers view results as controllable. Low achievers do not. There is no point in working hard if you don't believe hard work affects the results.

4. Attribution is a learned behavior. We learn it from copying what we hear around us: listening to our parents, watching TV, playing with friends, and talking to teachers and coaches. Like any subject, we can learn to attribute better.

5. Attribution can become a habit. Any learned behavior can be made into a habit. By creating a habit of attributing like a high achiever, we can influence the way we understand our results and set future expectations. The better we do it, the more likely our thoughts will contribute to future success.

The way we talk about our performance affects the way we think about it. The more we repeat explanations that reinforce productive thoughts, *the more we will have those thoughts.*

Or to put it in the simplest terms: Talk better, think better. Think better, train better.

Green's Razor

You can create a strong attribution habit by following Green's Razor[37]: *Never attribute to talent or luck that which is adequately explained by effort.*

> *"Green's Razor: Never attribute to talent or luck that which is adequately explained by effort."*

When you talk about your results, force yourself to tell the story in terms of effort and preparation. Do the same about other people. Make this your default. Don't accept other explanations without overwhelming evidence.

It's not about being right (though more often than not, you will be). It's about being productive. It's about thinking better. And it's about creating a better environment for you and those around you.

As a parent, I think about this a lot. I have a daily opportunity to practice attribution when I speak with my children about their performance. We try to focus as much as possible on the role their effort plays, and what they can do differently to prepare

---

[37] This is a modified take on Hanlon's Razor, which states: "Never attribute to malice that which is adequately explained by stupidity."

better. When something is too hard, we try to figure out if that's really the case. We assume they have plenty of talent to do what they want.

In the end, I'm not concerned about them being perfect. I want them to build the attribution habits of a high achiever.

As a coach, teammate, friend or parent, you have the opportunity to do the same for others in your life.

5: Growth Mindset: Nothing About You is Fixed

We have a tendency to admire talent. Or, more accurately, we have a tendency to admire greatness, and to confuse greatness with great talent. We see what people are able to do and we think, "Wow, they must be special." We attribute that special ability to their talent, something fixed and unchangeable within each of us.

The bookshelves are littered with biographies of geniuses, savants, phenoms, champions and "born leaders": Jordan. Tiger. Mozart. Picasso. Churchill. Bieber.[38] And let's not forget about the great runners: Elliot. Ryun. Prefontaine. Dibaba. Gebrselassie. Radcliffe. Kipchoge. Meb.

They probably do have something that most of us don't. But we can't know this simply by looking at their performances. A performance shows us a person's ability at a specific point in

---

[38] You know you've made it when you only go by one name.

time. And ability is different from talent. Ability is talent molded by effort over time.

> *"Ability is not talent. It is talent molded by effort over time."*

OTP #4: Ability is a variable, not a constant. The harder you work, the more able you become.

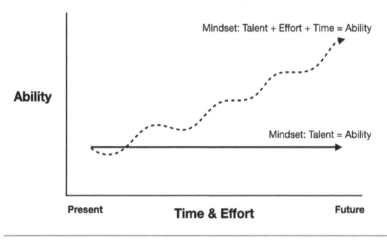

Fig 26 - Ability is not defined by talent. It is defined by talent + effort + time.

Meb Keflezighi is talented. How talented is impossible to say. I doubt he's the most physically talented runner I've ever met. He is, however, the hardest working, most disciplined runner I've ever seen.

At UCLA, he ran twice a day, did insane numbers of sit-ups, stretched religiously, underwent pre- and post-workout treatment regularly, ate healthy food, slept enough, and to top it off, he studied hard in all of his classes.[39]

---

[39] He apparently had to read many texts twice because as a non-native speaker he didn't learn everything in one go.

Though he was already a three-time NCAA champion when I first met him, everything I heard from teammates was that Meb entered school with this work ethic and discipline. Twenty years later he's recently retired from competitive running as an Olympic silver-medalist and winner of the Boston and New York City marathons (amongst many other accolades).

Coach Larsen attributed Meb's Boston victory to his ability to maintain his form and efficiency all the way to the finish. He attributed it to 20 years of daily form drills. As he said to me, "No athlete in history has probably done more drills than Meb."[40]

When we talk about an athlete like Meb in terms of his genetic talent—"He has Eritrean genes!"—we discredit the real difference between Meb and us: Meb has worked smarter and harder than us over a twenty year period. His success wasn't preordained by the gods like a Greek hero. He took his talents and painstakingly developed them.

If anything, the talent that separates Meb from 99% of his competition is not physical. It is his passion, motivation, discipline, compulsion, obsession, whatever-you-want-to-call-it to do what is necessary, day in and day out. To build the world's most effective feedback loop and consistently get 100% out of it. The same applies for other "great talents."

Michael Jordan was cut from his high school varsity basketball team. He credits it with making him truly apply himself on the court for the first time. Mozart and Tiger were coached early and obsessively by their fathers. Picasso painted non-stop from the age of four, and deliberately put himself in environments that challenged him creatively. Churchill failed repeatedly before leading England during World War II. Bieber overcame that terrible haircut.

Looking back we see clearly their ability. We don't always acknowledge the hard work. Prodigies or not, their performances improved over years of constant hard work. The same goes for everyone at the top of their field.

---

[40] In an interview on the Go Be More Podcast on 7/24/2020.

Mindsets: Growth vs Fixed

I first heard about Professor Carol Dweck from an article about her work called "The Effort Effect".[41] She researches what she calls "mindsets."

Mindsets refer to how people view ability. Some people view ability as something that can be developed (what she terms the "growth" mindset), while others view it as something inherent that needs to be demonstrated (what she terms the "fixed" mindset).

If you have a **fixed mindset**, you assume your talent is defining your potential. As you remember from attribution theory, talent is the one factor that is both internal and fixed; it is inherent to you.

With a fixed mindset you won't believe there is any point to working hard, because it won't make a difference. On top of that, when you perform your result will be a reflection of you as a person. Success is a reflection of how special you are.

But the potential for failure carries risk. People with fixed mindsets also believe that failure demonstrates how special *they aren't*. And because ability is fixed, they can't do anything to change it. This leads to avoiding challenges, making excuses, and visibly "not caring" (devaluing the activity to make a potential poor performance less meaningful).

The opposite of the fixed mindset is the **growth mindset**. With a growth mindset you believe your ability can be developed with effort. When you encounter a challenge, you naturally assume you can overcome it. You just need to figure out how.

In general, the focus of a person with a growth mindset is on learning, developing, and improving. Dweck even argues that this mindset is what enables a person to stay passionate and engaged over a long period of time. And this makes sense. It's easy to love something when it's easy and everything is going well. But when we run into difficulties, when things aren't going well, we get through it by focusing on our improvement.

---

[41] The article was published on the Stanford Magazine in March 2007

Qualities

Mindset	Focus	Performance	Cultivates
Fixed	Demonstration	Reflection of self	Fear of failure; Avoiding challenges
Growth	Development	Reflection of effort put in	Passion for activity you are doing

Fig 27 - A growth mindset cultivates a healthier attitude about performance, which leads to passion; a fixed mindset leads to a fear of failure

This isn't to say achievements aren't prized by those of us with a growth mindset. We can be just as competitive as anyone else. But the achievements are symbols of the growth and hard work it took to get them, not reflections of who we are.

This leads to an interesting outcome: people with a fixed mindset *want to achieve greatness* much more than those with a growth mindset because they want to demonstrate their inherent greatness; but it is often the person with a growth mindset that *actually achieves greatness*, because they maintained their engagement and put in the necessary work.

How We Measure Success

Let's take a short detour before we come back to growth vs fixed mindsets. We need to talk about how we measure success in the first place.

We see excellence all around us. People who have reached a point in their sport/job/career/whatever where they are recognized as "the best."

Norm-referenced excellence is success judged against external benchmarks: time, place, competition, market share, records, endorsements, etc. It's the way we "objectively" determine how good someone is. The person who runs faster, or scores more points, or makes more money is the one who had a better career. This is what every GOAT[42] discussion boils down to.

Norm-referenced performances are a valid and important measure of ability. As money enters the equation, they become even more important.

We need to keep straight what they are and what they are not. Norm-referenced excellence is:

- what we commonly refer to when we speak about "excellence"
- easily noticeable; this type of excellence stands out
- typically qualified by external factors (especially location and age)
- what ultimately leads to fame and fortune,[43] and
- what the Olympics and professional leagues are a showcase for

You've seen the headline: Jane Fastwitch runs fastest 5k time for a 70 year-old in the history of Smalltown, USA; now holds 46 local age group records!

We can't all be Jane Fastwitch. Thankfully we don't need to be. Because while norm-referenced performances are how we typically view the world, there is another, equally legitimate way to evaluate ourselves: **self-referenced excellence**.

Self-referenced excellence is:

- an equally legitimate measure of excellence
- the measure that leads to pride and self-discovery
- typically qualified by internal factors (feelings, expectations)
- transferrable from one activity to another, and
- the way we judge whether a performance was optimal or not

Looking at a time or place on the results sheet doesn't tell us the whole story. It doesn't account for how well you executed,

---

[42] Greatest Of All Time

[43] Or for most runners: local news coverage and free shoes

		Norm-Referenced	Self-Referenced
Time Period	Short-term	Fast Time Winner of Race	Improvement Optimal Performance
	Long-term	Champion All-Time List Hall of Fame	Fulfillment Realize Potential

Fig 28 - Norm-referenced typically focuses on comparing, whereas self-referenced focuses on context

how you felt during and after, and whether your performance could have been better under the circumstances.

For example, who do you think feels better: the pro who cruises and wins a local race, or the amateur who finishes in 10th place with a new personal best? I guarantee you it's the amateur.

Why? Because the winner didn't (need to) run an excellent race. The person who finished 10th did.

Mindsets, Measuring Success, and Making Leaps

Making a leap requires working hard to sustain your momentum over time, and allowing small consistent gains to compound until they result in a dramatic improvement. You can already see how this aligns much closer to a growth mindset and self-referenced evaluation.

If you have a fixed mindset, the idea that you can make a leap is absurd. Your talent will always limit your potential to improve. You lean on norm-referenced criteria, because those demonstrate your talent relative to others. If your performances are good, you're happy. If not, you start looking for excuses.

A growth mindset emphasizes improvement, progress, and the ability to change. Self-referenced criteria become your main focus when evaluating performance. Performing to your expectations become just as important as the finishing time or place.

Qualities

Mindset		Focus	Performance	Cultivates
	Fixed	Norm-Referenced Achievement	Indication of Relative Position	Desire to Be Great
	Growth	Self-Referenced Achievement	Indication of Progress	Actual Greatness

Fig 29 - Norm-referenced focus leads to a desire to be great; self-referenced leads to actual greatness

Having a growth mindset doesn't automatically lead to making a leap. But it is a way of thinking that justifies your effort and produces better results. Our brains are prediction factories. Athletes who adopt a growth mindset produce better, more realistic expectations about what is possible. And they are more likely to do the work to achieve it.

"Athletes who adopt a growth mindset produce better, more realistic expectations about what is possible."

Three Big Benefits

Focusing on self-referenced performance has three other benefits that help to cultivate a growth mindset.

First, it forces you to think about context, not comparisons. Context requires understanding the conditions at the time, and evaluating process before results.

Here are two descriptions for my PAC-10 cross country championships performance my sophomore year.

- Norm-referenced: Everybody kicked my ass today.
- Self-referenced: I was caught off guard by the fast initial pace. I struggled mid-way with a side stitch. I couldn't main-

tain my pace after that. I got frustrated and lost focus. I rallied a little at the end but it had little impact on my final place.

There's nothing to learn from the norm-referenced evaluation. The self-referenced evaluation creates opportunities for improvement. The same would have been true if the results were good.

Another benefit is that self-referenced achievements are often transferrable. When you connect your preparation to your results, you reinforce the benefits of preparation in all areas of your life. When you learn to think in terms of progress instead of place, you approach new problems differently.

When we start something new, we typically suck at it. When we get a new job, we have a lot to learn. When we learn a new skill, it takes hours of practice. Focusing on self-referenced achievements is what enables us to put in the necessary work without judging ourselves too harshly.

Lastly, self-referenced evaluation lets you try new things, experiment, and test yourself. It frees you to fail with purpose.

In my senior year, I competed in an indoor 3000m championships in Flagstaff, Arizona. I considered myself the top runner in the field and it was a great opportunity to win a title. Given the altitude in Flagstaff, we designed a race plan that emphasized conserving myself as long as possible. Then the race went out incredibly, embarrassingly, unexpectedly slow. Slower than our warm-up pace slow.

With about half the race left, I got impatient and tried to run away from everyone. I opened a big lead. Then, as we feared when we crafted the race plan, the altitude caught up with me. I got caught in the last stretch and finished second.

So was it a mistake? Yes, but not because I finished second. It was a mistake because I didn't stick with my plan, and I didn't have a good backup plan for that situation. At the time, I felt like I screwed up my best chance at winning a title. Now many years removed, the title is irrelevant to me. I took a chance and, from a norm-referenced point of view, it didn't work out. Oh well.

Trying new things may not lead to the same norm-referenced success. But it teaches you about your abilities and gives you valuable experience for future races. Unfortunately, you'll never try if you are focused solely on norm-referenced success. When you put your performances in context and focus on process over results, you give yourself permission to take bold risks.

Spotting a Fixed Mindset

You may be thinking at this point that anyone who runs competitively must already have a growth mindset, because the improvement-to-effort connection is so obvious. But that's not the case. As I wrote in the intro, I approached running with a fixed mindset and my success made it worse.

I had a teammate in high school who was the star on his junior high team. He'd long been told how gifted he was. He barely cracked our top seven, though. It had nothing to do with his talent. We were a strong squad and he was young.

After a while he slacked in practice or sometimes didn't come, and he always had an excuse for why he wasn't performing well. He eventually quit.

At the time, I thought he was just lazy. Looking back, I no longer believe that was his problem. He had a fixed mindset about running. He believed success would come naturally for him if he had "real" talent. It made him look bad (and feel bad) to not be the star, so he built excuses into his training for a while, lost enthusiasm and then eventually quit.

I've always been convinced he would have been one of our top runners if he had committed himself. At the time, we just didn't know how to diagnose the situation and help him change his mindset.

Here are a few tips for spotting a fixed mindset, in yourself or others:

- You view success and failure exclusively as norm-referenced
- You feel shame after poor performances
- You blame lack of talent or bad luck for poor performances

- You act like a poor performance isn't something you care about
- You emphasize how easy a good performance was (thus emphasizing your talent)
- You engage when successful and detach and disengage when not

You may recognize some of these in yourself, your teammates, or your athletes (if you are a coach). Just like with attribution theory, some people have a growth mindset in one area and a fixed mindset in another. I've seen athletes that appear to have a growth mindset about middle distances and a fixed mindset about anything 5k and over. People are complicated.

Fixing a Fixed Mindset

The natural question is, how fixed are fixed mindsets? Thankfully, they're not!

Dweck makes the argument that different mindsets are often the product of our environment. We can change them with some simple exercises. Which allows us to write this sentence: Fixed mindsets aren't fixed; they can be fixed. (Thank you. Thank you.)

The first method I call the **Reframing Approach:** Attribute success to effort and preparation. De-emphasize talent.

People with a fixed mindset attribute their performance to their perceived talent. This starts early in life. Many parents praise their children's intelligence and talent as a way to build their confidence. The goal is a good one, but it reinforces fixed mindset thinking.

To take a simple example, many people believe math is something some people "get" and others don't. Just yesterday, a mom in my neighborhood told me she's "not a numbers person." Describing herself this way to her kids *will inevitably affect the way her kids view the world.* Some people can do math and others can't.

Imagine your child is doing well at math and you praise her for being talented. She will get a boost in confidence at that moment. But what happens when she later encounters something difficult, that doesn't come easy? She will be in danger of thinking she can't do it. If she could it would be easier.

An environment focused on effort-based results will foster a growth mindset in every aspect of life. This includes playing sports, learning languages, writing code, acting, playing instruments, managing people, and even drawing.

The second I call the **Analogy Approach:** find an area where people have a fixed mindset and demonstrate that it shouldn't be.

What is the one field that is most closely associated with talent? Art, right? When we see an amazing painting, the first thing we think is, "I don't even understand how they could make this."

Artists are naturals, geniuses, born with a paintbrush in hand. And it's true that all great artists are talented. But that doesn't mean you and I can't learn to draw or paint at a high level.

Look at the before and after pictures of people who have taken Betty Edwards' course on drawing.[44] You will realize how much of an artist's ability is in the training and practice, and not just talent. It's not that we can't draw, it's that we haven't learned properly.

> ### "Often it's not that we can't do something. It's that we haven't learned properly."

This example really hit me. I always assumed I could improve at running, but I also believed I was talented. I had never been successful with some other things, however, including art, music, and learning languages. But seeing the before and after pictures from Edwards' course clearly refuted my fixed mindset about art.

The growth mindset is tied to attribution theory. High achievers tend to have a growth mindset and attribute their performance to their effort. The causation goes both ways. A growth

---

44 http://drawright.com/before-after/

mindset naturally lends itself to "high achiever" attribution, but choosing to attribute like a high achiever can also cultivate a growth mindset.

Here are a few ideas to help you cultivate a growth mindset.

- Keep reading, the next chapter ties in directly
- Talk about the growth mindset with others
- Read an article that discusses how someone improved with effort
- Think about something you have improved at by doing it over time (it can be anything)
- Ask someone about how they prepare for challenges and why it works
- When you hear about someone's talent, assume it is only part of the story; ask about the effort they put in

These aren't difficult. You can do them in an instant. The more you do them, the more you will reinforce your growth mindset.

Key Takeaways

1. Norm-referenced goals are measured against external factors. Self-referenced goals are measured against internal factors. Excellence is often measured against norm-referenced factors, but great athletes base their training on self-referenced factors.

2. People with a Fixed mindset believe that talent is something to be demonstrated, whereas those with a Growth mindset believe that ability is developed through effort.

3. A Fixed mindset can be developed into a Growth mindset through the Reframing Approach—emphasizing effort and preparation—and the Analogy Approach—finding an area that appears to be fixed and showing that it isn't.

6: Self-Efficacy: Systematically Believing in Yourself

It's one thing to be engaged and responsible and have a growth mindset. It's another to believe it matters for the specific task at hand. Do you believe that all the effort you are putting into your training will pay off?[45]

The next Optimal Training Principle deals with **self-efficacy**: *the belief that you can accomplish something based on the effort you put into it.*

Difficult goals are hard to achieve, and the road is neither straight nor smooth.[46] We don't undertake difficult journeys unless we have confidence we can reach the end. That confidence comes from our belief in ourselves and the plan we will follow.

---

[45] Or that your studies will result in better grades? Or that you can learn a new skill to succeed in your career? Or that your efforts can improve your relationships?

[46] Spoiler: it's bumpy as hell.

We can boost this belief.

OTP #5: Self-efficacy is a fundamental ingredient to overcoming obstacles and achieving success.

This principle directly ties together the Momentum Model and Attribution Theory. In order to make a leap, we need to maintain enough motivation to overcome the negative forces and obstacles in our way. And attribution theory showed us that high achievers attribute both their successes and failures to their effort.

It follows then, that self-efficacy—believing your effort affects your outcomes for a specific task—is a positive force to help you achieve your goals. In fact, self-efficacy may be even more fundamental. Without it you won't try in the first place.

Self-efficacy is not Self-esteem

Self-efficacy is not self-esteem. Self-esteem is an evaluation of your own worth. It's how you feel about yourself. You can have high self-efficacy and low self-esteem, or low self-efficacy and high self-esteem. The two are distinct.

	Measure of	Focus on	Valuable for
Self-Esteem	Self-worth	Feelings	Feeling good about yourself
Self-Efficacy	Ability to succeed	Outcomes	Accomplishing difficult tasks

Fig 30 - Self-esteem focuses on how you feel; self-efficacy focus on what you can achieve

Self-efficacy focuses on potential outcomes. Self-esteem focuses on feelings. Which brings us to another distinction. Feelings are not attitudes. Feelings deal with how sensitive you are, usually in the form of a reaction to whatever is happening in the moment. They are fleeting. Feelings change with the circumstances.

Attitudes are mental positions from which we view the world. Attitudes are foundational. They can be changed, but it's hard. Self-efficacy is an attitude. It's a way of viewing the world. Feeling lazy is one thing. It's fairly easy to overcome, and either way it eventually passes. Having a lazy attitude is quite another. It affects literally everything we do.

I want you to feel good about yourself, and I want you to have high self-esteem.[47] But for the purposes of your training, you need to have high self-efficacy. High self-efficacy leads to greatness. High self-esteem leads to contentment regardless of the outcome.

The 4 (+2) Experiences that Increase Self-Efficacy

There are four (plus two) types of experience that contribute to our self-efficacy. That's right. Four (plus two). Let's go through them in order of importance.

		Type of Factor	
		Internal	External
Effect on Self-Efficacy	High	Personal Experience	Vicarious Experience
	Low	Physiological; Visualization; Faith	Social Persuasion

Fig 31 - The 4(+2) ways of increasing self-efficacy. Personal experience is the strongest boost, followed by Vicarious experience

[47] I agree with Stuart Smalley: You're good enough. You're smart enough. And gosh darn it, people like you.

1. Personal Experience: Seeing actual improvement or success

If you've done something once, you will believe you can do it again. If you've come close, you're going to feel confident that you can achieve it with a little more work.

It doesn't take much to boost your self-efficacy. Feeling great at the end of a hard workout can do it. So can staying close to a better runner longer than usual (even if they beat you at the end). Or beating someone with a similar personal best to the person you are really aiming to beat. These experiences make us feel more confident that our hard work will pay off.

But it doesn't even have to be an objective experience. Sometimes you need to see how much effort you have to give.

My junior year we came down from two weeks of altitude training at Mammoth Lakes and we attempted to implement a team race plan at a local invitational. The plan was to stick together for 5k before moving up as much as possible over the final 3k. At 5k, I was in 50th place or so, and at the end of the race I finished 6th. My time wasn't fast and a couple of the guys who beat me weren't that good.[48]

The results didn't matter. This race changed me. The process of going from 50th to 6th was grueling. In the final 800 meters I was redlining. In the final 400 meters there was another runner just close enough that I sprinted as hard as possible to catch him at the end. I hit the line and then I semi-blacked out.[49]

I remember little of the next hour, just feeling light-headed as I walk-jogged my warm-down. I couldn't eat, had a pounding headache, every muscle ached, and when I got home I threw up and fell asleep on the couch.

---

[48] I actually don't remember the exact course, my final time, or who beat me. I can't find the results anywhere. And yet on some measure I feel this is the most important race I ever ran.

[49] I greyed out? I never fainted, just lost all coherence for a short time.

So why was it so important? It showed me *how hard I can push myself*. I had never felt that way before (and I didn't want to ever again). But from that day forward in every race, no matter how bad I felt, *I knew I could go harder*.

The most important tool you have to improve your self-efficacy are your personal experiences. Use them.

"The most important tool you have to improve your self-efficacy are your personal experiences. Use them."

2. Vicarious Experience: Seeing someone else achieve something

The second best way to boost your self-efficacy is to see *someone you relate to* accomplish something. When Roger Bannister broke the 4-minute barrier for the mile, everyone who felt they were his equal immediately believed they could break it, too.

It's best if the people you observe are similar to you. If you don't see yourself as being roughly equal, it is easy to pass off their accomplishments as being due to their talent or situation. But seeing someone *just like you* achieve a goal or make a leap can be motivating.

In the 1999 NCAA West Regional meet, an athlete named Jon Doroski finished in the top 25 and qualified as an individual for the NCAA Championships. I finished around 50th. Prior to my summer vacation, I had the following exchange with my new coach, Eric Peterson:

Me: "There's no reason Jon Doroski can make it to NCAAs and I can't."

Coach: "Bullshit. He was ready to do it and you aren't. That's the reason. So how are you going to change that?"

Me: "Umm..."

Doroski had made a leap that season and I hadn't. But "if he can do it, I can, too" is a powerful idea. We agreed it wasn't a question of talent, but of readiness (preparation and effort). "If Doroski can do it, I can, too" carried me through my summer training and set me up to make a leap later that year.

> ### *"'If he can do it, I can, too,' is a powerful idea.*
> ### *Use it."*

The other time that stands out had to do with a good runner making a big leap. Peter Gilmore–who went on to run a 2:12 marathon–ran for UC Berkeley and made a big leap in the PAC-10. Peter was always a good runner, but he was never a *great* runner like Meb, Bernard Lagat, Abdi Abdirahman, and Brad Hauser.[50]

Peter Gilmore was relatable. My teammate Will and I talked about Peter on our runs. Will had beaten him in high school, and I was running as fast as Will. We could imagine beating Peter. We literally said to each other: "If Gilmore can do it, we can, too!"

Were we as talented as Peter Gilmore? I don't know and it doesn't matter. We believed we were. So his results became a proxy for what our results could be. And that got me to increase my effort, after which my improvement led to even more effort and so on.[51]

There is also great value in studying people who have achieved true greatness, but how you study them is important. You have to avoid the **"talent trap."**

The "talent trap" is an attribution error, where we see an amazing result and assume it is primarily due to talent. You find yourself saying things like, "Of course Meb is great. He's African!" Or, "Of course Matt Centrowitz could win a gold medal. His dad ran 13:15 for 5k!"

---

[50] All Olympians who competed in the conference at that time. The Pac-10 was stacked!

[51] Full disclosure: We never achieved Peter's level, but we both made significant improvements that year.

To avoid the talent trap, remember Green's Razor: "Never attribute to talent that which is adequately explained by effort."

Talent is always there. If you look for talent, you'll find it. Especially in the best of the best. But if you look at an excellent individual through the lens of their efforts, you can learn a lot. You'll see that Meb and Centro (and every other champion) have worked incredibly hard for an incredibly long time.

You can't control talent. You can only control effort. Focus on *their* effort to evaluate whether yours stacks up.

"Focus on great athletes' effort to evaluate whether yours stacks up."

3. Social Persuasion: Being told you can (or can't) do something

Personal experience and vicarious experience are the most reliable ways to increase self-efficacy. But social persuasion–someone you trust saying you can do something–can also be effective. Especially for those with limited experience. The key is that your trust in the person telling you is stronger than whatever negative beliefs you hold.

Social persuasion can happen implicitly or explicitly. In my first year running, we went camping as a team. I had a particularly good run on the last day, where I ran away from our top runner. On the drive home, my coach Bob Grove looked at me in the rear-view mirror and said, "I think you can be one of the best runners in the league this year."

That was enough for me. He would know, he's the coach! I trained and raced the rest of the year *assuming* I should be one of the best, and ended up 3rd in our league championships.

Explicit feedback is always present on a running team. Coaches and teammates encourage us to practice hard, to go for difficult goals. This is important. But it's also important to realize when the feedback is happening implicitly or indirectly.

If you feel like you're being held back, like others don't believe in you, it's important to address it. You want to keep your momentum and your positive feedback loop as strong as possible. You don't want to be held back by the goals you don't set, the practices you don't do, or the competition you don't face.

You need to talk openly with your coach, because your goals and expectations need to be aligned for you to have success. This is your responsibility.

Being held back in the moment isn't always a bad thing. Neither is being upset about it. But it's important to have someone reminding us that it's only because we're not ready *right now*. With hard work, we can be ready in the future.

4. Physiological Factors: How you respond to your body's natural reactions

Your body will have a natural reaction to stress (getting butterflies before a race, for example). That reaction can either increase or decrease your self-efficacy. It is normal to get nervous before a race. Everyone does. But some athletes deal with that feeling better than others.

I trained with an NCAA Champion who threw up before every race...even minor dual meets. But he learned it didn't affect his performance, and he modified his pre-race routine to account for it.[52] Even extreme nervousness can be overcome.

Most distance runners share one particular physiological response that makes them well-suited to the sport: the ability to tolerate discomfort. If discomfort makes you miserable, you won't put in the necessary work to be a great runner.

Some people just like running. It makes them feel good and they feel better after a run. Others don't. If you're wired to enjoy something, you are more likely to get out the door and do it.

---

[52] Typical pre-race conversation:
"Where's...?"
"Toilet."
"Oh, right."

Of the four canonical factors, physiological factors have the least impact on your self-efficacy, but they are worth knowing about. Young runners in particular are prone to misinterpreting their body and lowering their goals or expectations.

+2. Other Internal Factors: Visualization and Faith

Neither of these are part of the self-efficacy "canon." But there is an argument for both. Especially visualization. Many great athletes employ visualization as part of their training program: imagining hitting particular splits, imagining the race unfolding in various ways and how to respond, or imagining maintaining great form all through the finishing sprint.

Visualization acts as a virtual personal experience. It's not truly personal experience because you haven't done it. It's not vicarious because it's not based on someone else. It's...unique. And it can boost your self-efficacy in many circumstances.

Visualization is related to planning. There is a saying in the military that applies: "Plans are worthless but planning is everything."[53]

When we create a plan we predict what could happen and decide how we should react. But knowing you should do something and being ready to do it are different things. Visualization turns something you haven't done into a "feels like I've done it before" action. It primes us to act.

"Visualization turns something you haven't done into a 'feels like I've done it before' action. It primes us to act."

You can't predict how everything will go, but you can plan for the most likely situations. What if they go out fast? What if they go out slow? What if somebody makes a move early? It helps to visualize how you want to respond in each case. The likelihood

---

[53] This is attributed to Dwight D. Eisenhower.

that your race will go exactly as you expected is small. But the more scenarios you've considered, the more prepared you'll be.

Visualization is most powerful when we only get one attempt. My favorite example of this is free-soloist Alex Honnold, who climbed El Capitan in Yosemite *without ropes*. In his TED talk,[54] he talks about spending *years* visualizing the four hour (!), 3,000 foot vertical climb to the point that he could see in his mind every hand hold and how he would successfully navigate them.

In his case, visualization wasn't the only factor. He gained personal experience via practice runs (with ropes) and he free-soloed other places to gain experience. Physiologically he benefits from not being afraid of heights and from just a touch of wacko. But if he failed, he'd be dead. He needed to believe he could do it. Visualization was critical for him.

Running a race isn't life or death but you often only get one chance. The more important the race, the more you need to believe in your ability to execute your plan. Visualization is particularly useful for this.

Faith is different. Faith is tied to self-efficacy when you believe that your training has a higher purpose, and that your hard work will help you achieve it. In this sense, faith is a motivator. Somewhat similar to social persuasion, but coming from inside you.

Religious faith isn't necessary to be a champion runner, but it can help if it makes you believe your goal is meaningful and achievable. On the flip side, if you are convinced you will achieve it regardless, it could hinder your willingness to plan strategically.

Faith tied to effort and preparation can enhance our self-efficacy. Faith tied to results, not so much. Focus your faith to make it work for you.

Persistence

I like this quote by Calvin Coolidge, the 2nd most quotable US president:

---

[54] Search for Alex Honnold on TED.com

Nothing in the world can take the place of persistence. Talent will not; nothing is more common than unsuccessful men with talent. Genius will not; unrewarded genius is almost a proverb. Education will not; the world is full of educated failures. Persistence and determination alone are omnipotent.
- Calvin Coolidge, former U.S. President

Persistence is the ability to continue in the face of adversity and failure without giving up. The Finn's call it *sisu* and consider it the most important indicator of future success. Across the board, in all walks of life, persistence is the one quality to which most successful people attribute their success. They stuck with it longer. They outworked the competition.

But remember, persistence does not mean sticking with the same plan despite poor results. Persistence is sticking with the same goal, and finding the plan that achieves it.

"Persistence is sticking with the same goal, and finding the plan that achieves it."

Persistence is the natural by-product of the previous four Optimal Training Principles. If you are engaged, responsible, believe you can improve and have high self-efficacy for the task at hand, you will *want* to work hard, *feel you need* to work hard, and *believe* that your hard work matters.

It becomes less a question of whether you can and more whether you care enough.

Key Takeaways

1. Self-efficacy is the belief in what you can achieve based on the effort you put into a task.

2. You can improve your self-efficacy through various experiences. The most effective are personal experiences and vicarious experiences.

3. Persistence is pursuing a goal despite obstacles and difficulties, and changing tactics as necessary to achieve it. It is both a by-product and a contributor to self-efficacy.

Spotlight: The 80/20 Rule

Baseball legend Yogi Berra once said, "Baseball is 90 percent mental. The other half is physical." He was right. Running is, too. The 80/20 Rule explains why.

What Is the 80/20 Rule?

The 80/20 Rule began as an observation by Italian academic Vilfredo Pareto in the early 1900s. He was studying the relationship between land ownership and population, and he discovered that 20% of Italians owned 80% of the land.

Over time economists, sociologists and business people have noticed countless similar relationships:

- 20% of people own 80% of the world's wealth
- 20% of menu items generate 80% of revenues
- 20% of employees generate 80% of an organization's productivity
- 20% of words make up 80% of a language's usage

- 20% of software bugs cause 80% of crashes
- 20% of our friends generate 80% of our positive memories
- 20% of cities account for 80% of the global population
- 20% of training activities account for 80% of success

I find it easiest to visualize using the below chart[55]:

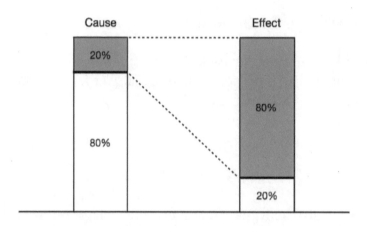

Fig 32 - The 80/20 Rule illustrates that inputs and outputs are not proportional

We can see three clear ideas in this image:

1. Cause and effect are related but distinct
2. A small number of activities generate the majority of our results
3. A large number of activities generate a small portion of our results

What we do and the results we achieve are not *proportional*. When we can measure it, we can determine the exact relationship. But even when we can't, the 80/20 Rule gives us a simple mental model for assuming the relationship.

---

[55] These column diagrams are inspired by the work of Michael Simmons.

In running, time and effort are your main constraints. Is it better to spend your time running or weight lifting? Sleeping or stretching? Eating healthy or meditating?

It's obvious that not all activities are equally effective. But it's not always obvious how much more effective one activity is than another. The 80/20 Rule gives us a useful approximation.

Do the Max or Do the Min?

The key question for each activity is, "How should I get the most out of this?" I propose a different answer for top-20% activities and rest-of-80% activities.

> *"The key question for each activity is, 'How should I get the most out of this?'"*

For top-20% activities, your efforts create huge returns. Therefore, you should aim to get as much as possible out of them. You want to max them out. These activities include anything core to achieving your goals: practice, recovery, treatment.

Rest-of-80% activities play a minor but still important role in our success. We can't achieve our potential if we only focus on top-20% activities, but spending lots of time and effort on the rest-of-80% doesn't get us proportional benefits.[56]

For these activities, you want to do the minimum necessary. Your strategy should be to keep them as positive as possible *without putting any extra effort into them.* We want to systematize these activities.[57]

Five Insights

---

[56] The economics term for this is *diminishing marginal returns.* More effort results in fewer and fewer returns.

[57] We will cover this in depth in Chapter 9.

1. The 80/20 Rule is not a law of physics. It's a mental model. Like all mental models, it's a shortcut for making assumptions about how the world works.

2. The relationship is not always 80/20. The actual relationship could be any combination of numbers: 90/10, 70/10, or even 95/25 (the numbers do not need to add up to 100).

3. Not all areas of life can be explained by the 80/20 Rule. Some things are normally distributed, like talent, intelligence, and personality traits. The top 20% of runners do not contain 80% of all the running talent in the world.[58]

4. 80/20 thinking is a tool for prioritizing. The appropriate time to use the 80/20 Rule is when you have a scarce resource (like time or energy) and a criteria for prioritizing it (effectiveness, joy, profit, etc).

5. It can be easy to take it too far. If all the choices are too similar, then the 80/20 Rule doesn't help. If your goal is to eat healthy, then you can't use 80/20 thinking to decide between broccoli and spinach. Use another criteria to make that decision, like texture or "sticks in your teethiness."

Using the 80/20 Rule in Training

From a Momentum Model point of view, the 80/20 Rule helps us identify the big arrows from the little ones. It gives us a rough guess as to how much bigger some arrows can be.

Positive 80/20: The quickest way to improve is to strengthen your biggest and strongest arrows. Get engaged more. Take more responsibility. Get more sleep. Emphasize your effort and ability to improve.

---

[58] It is reasonable, however, to assume that the top 20% most talented athletes will receive at least 80% of the money/fame/respect/etc.

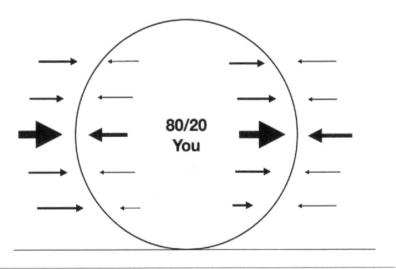

Fig 33 · The 80/20 Rule can help us identify the relative strength (and importance) of the arrows in the Momentum Model

For external forces, find the people you train best with and train with them more often. Do the workouts that energize and motivate you. Shift your responsibilities so you can do them when you have the appropriate energy (early in the morning, later in the afternoon).

"Pushing harder is essential. But it's equally important not to be held back."

Negative 80/20: Flip the 80/20 Rule around and look at the negative behaviors holding you back. You always want to be moving forward, so you must avoid anything that can stop your progress completely. Activities that lead to injury are top of the list.

Many of us spend too much time with people or in environments whose priorities don't align to our own. Family members, roommates, colleagues, and friends can all have agendas that conflict with our goals. Figure out how to use an 80/20 approach to reduce their negative impact.

We make a leap by creating and sustaining momentum. Pushing harder is essential. But it's equally important not to be held back.

90% Mental...Half Physical

Let's quickly come back to Yogi Berra's famous quote: "Baseball is 90 percent mental. The other half is physical."

Whether he meant it or not, his quote illustrates the insight underlying the 80/20 Rule. The drivers of success in baseball (and running) can be mental or physical. The mental "half" drives 90% of the results. Think better, train better.

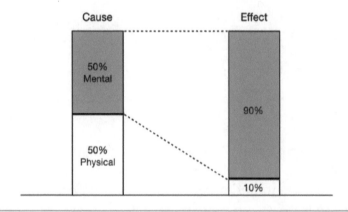

Fig 34 - The 80/20 Rule explains why Yogi Berra is right (whether he knew it or not)

7: Causation: All Success Starts in the Same Place

et's recap briefly. The goal of our training is to get better. We train better when we think better about training. And when we train the right way, we get *exponentially* better: we make a leap.

Improvement is not linear. When we create positive feedback loops in our training, it leads to exponential improvement. We create strong feedback loops by being engaged and responsible. This enables us to find our 80/20 activities and improve them. A growth mindset, a self-referenced focus and high self-efficacy give us the belief that we can accomplish our goals if we are persistent.

These attitudes are the foundation of our training. The next Optimal Training Principle helps bridge the gap between our attitudes and our behaviors.

OTP #6: All behavior is caused. All causation is mental. We become what we think about most of the time.

Scientists who study long-term memory break it up into two types: Declarative (also called Explicit) and Procedural (also called Implicit). Declarative memory deals with things we recall consciously, like remembering a phone number or the ingredients to a recipe. Procedural memory concerns things we do unconsciously, like riding a bike or driving home from the supermarket.

	Thoughts	Trade-off	Also called
Explicit (Declarative)	Conscious, Voluntary	Effective, but Inefficient	Calculated Deliberate Intentional
Implicit (Procedural)	Unconscious, Involuntary	Efficient, but can be Ineffective	Muscle memory Spontaneous Automatic

Fig 35 · Understanding which of our behaviors are Explicit or Implicit can help us do them better

This division is useful for thinking about our daily routines as well.

We do the majority of our routines without thinking about them. We are on auto-pilot. For example, I have an empty cereal bowl sitting next to me and I don't remember taking any single bite. Almost every aspect of my breakfast routine is procedural.[59]

This isn't random. It's a survival mechanism. Thinking hard uses a lot of energy. Competitive chess players are known to burn as many calories as athletes at major competitions.

---

[59] This reminds me of a funny example of how procedural behavior can go wrong. When I was in high school I woke up early and in a kind of stupor began to pour myself a bowl of cereal. Instead of pouring the milk into my bowl I poured it directly into the cereal box. When auto-pilot goes wrong!

Our ability to navigate the day *without* thinking hard allows us to keep a reserve of mental energy, the same energy we draw from to exert willpower. This mental energy is so important we've developed what I call the **law of conservation of mental energy**: if we can do something without thinking, we will.

> *"The law of conservation of mental energy: if we* *can* *do something without thinking, we* ***will.****"*

When we learn a new skill or adopt a new behavior, we do it *explicitly*. But concentrating on it in this way requires a lot of willpower. Over enough time the skill becomes second nature and we begin to do it Implicitly, which increases our efficiency and conserves our mental energy.

What determines how efficiently and effectively we can do something? According to Anders Ericsson, who has studied expert performance for 40 years, it is our "mental representation" for that activity.

Understanding Mental Representations

In order to master any skill, we need to create a "mental representation" of how that skill is expertly performed. Ericsson defines a mental representation as "a mental structure that corresponds to an object, an idea, a collection of information, or anything else, concrete or abstract, that the brain is thinking about."[60] In other words, the way we think about something.

To do something well, we need to first have a well-defined understanding of what differentiates "well done" versus "poorly done." The simplest way to understand this is probably with music. In order to play a song on the piano, you need to have a clear understanding of what a well-played version of the song sounds like. Then you can compare your performance to your "mental representation."

---

[60] From his book: *Peak: Secrets from the New Science of Expertise*

Experts have incredibly well-defined mental representations. Beginners typically do not.

The quality and detail of your mental representation affects your ability to do it well. Someone who has never heard a song might be able to recognize it when it is being played, but not judge the quality.

In contrast, someone who has heard it many times, practiced it for hours, and identified all the difficult transitions will be more likely to play it at a high level. An expert pianist's mental representation will include subtle details such as the need to move their entire hand to a new position in order to smoothly play an upcoming combination of notes.

Let's put this in a running perspective. Imagine two athletes of equal ability entered to run the New York City marathon. The first is running her debut marathon. The other has run many marathons, including New York City a couple times.

NYC Marathon Mental Representation

	Distance	Course	Scenarios	Other Factors
Debut Marathoner	Never raced before	First time	Hoping it goes to plan	Best guess
Experienced Pro	Lots of experience	Many previous races	Ready for anything	Best plan based on previous experience

Fig 36 - An experienced pro will have a better mental representation than a debut marathoner

An NYC marathon mental representation might include:
- A detailed understanding of the course
- The necessary pacing to hit the goal time
- The way their body should feel at that pace at each stage
- Who else is competing and how they are likely to run
- Various options for reacting to unexpected situations
- How much and when to drink or eat
- How the specific weather will affect their performance

- Knowing whether they can/should respond to a move mid-race
- What it feels like to red-line to avoid "hitting the wall"

We could probably come up with many more, related to optimal diet, sleep, clothing, etc. The fact is, running a marathon is not something most people do well on their first try. There are too many aspects that you can't "understand" until you've done it a couple times, no matter how good you are.

The same goes for any other distance. Understanding how to handle being boxed in, running from the front, being in a crowded stadium vs an empty one, pacing, when to start your sprint, maintaining your form as you get tired... The more defined your mental representation of an ideal race is, the more likely you will be to execute it.

Most of these aspects can be practiced, or at least anticipated and prepared for. But it requires a specific approach to practice that goes beyond finishing your workouts. (We'll cover this in detail next chapter.)

For now, it's enough to state that the more deeply you understand what you are trying to do, the more likely you are to do it well.

Considering Consideration

Every activity we undertake has a mental representation at its foundation. And I mean every activity, from chewing our food to playing Fortnite to falling asleep at night. We can group everything we do into three categories:
- **Never considered:** Things we do that are habits born out of...who knows, we just do them.
- **Actively considered:** Things we think carefully about every time we do them.
- **Previously considered:** Things we actively considered at some point in the past but don't actively consider now.

If we are eating cereal, then these distinctions probably don't matter. Despite what the spilled milk on my chin might say, my spoon to mouth form is good enough. Improving it isn't an 80/20 priority.

		Consideration		
		Actively	*Never*	*Previously*
Effect on Behavior	*Benefit*	Can create new effective behaviors	Potentially efficient	**Effective and efficient**
	Drawback	Highly inefficient	Potentially ineffective	Potentially ineffective (if circumstances have changed)

Fig 37 - Strive to have previously considered all of your important behaviors and habits

But if there are areas of your training you've never considered, then you are assuming they are optimal. That's a risky assumption.

There's a good chance you are doing ineffective things, but doing them efficiently. Stretching is a great example. I often see athletes race through a poorly designed stretching routine. It might be better than not stretching at all, but they typically think they are getting more out of it than they are.

At some point, you must revisit each area of your training to see if it can be improved. You are striving to do the most effective activities in the most efficient way. If you've never considered what you are doing, how can you be sure of either?

"At some point, you must revisit each area of your training to see if it can be improved."

Actively considering activities creates the opposite problem. The more you think about what you are doing, the more inefficiently you do it. You think slower, you question your default behavior, and you are more critical of your performance.

116

When I played basketball with my dad, just before a game-winning shot he liked to ask me whether I breathe in or out when I shoot. He knew that shooting is procedural and if he could get me thinking about my shot in a declarative way I'd be more likely to mess up.[61] In a clutch moment, procedural activities need to stay procedural.

You also don't want to be actively considering every behavior in your daily life. No one has the energy to live that way. But you have to do this occasionally. It is the only way to create more effective mental representations.

As you can see, you want to have every area of your training and lifestyle *that you aren't actively focused on improving* be in the "previously considered" category. When you do this diligently, you create the right habits (high effectiveness) and you do them the right way (high efficiency).

I saw this first hand when I tried to improve my running form. My natural form was to run with my shoulders a bit scrunched and my arms a bit tight, not unlike a skinny T-Rex. At the end of a 10k race, my shoulders would fatigue and affect my stride. We worked hard to retrain my muscles so that I could relax my arms.

During this time, running became a declarative exercise for me. I had to think about my form constantly. I wasn't just trying to hit interval times, but hit them while maintaining perfect form. Eventually my more "relaxed" shoulders began to feel natural and I stopped thinking about them with every stride. I was back to procedural.

Our mental representations affect the quality of our effort. How much we've considered each activity affects our mental representations. It starts in our heads.

From Passionate to Meh

We all feel a different degree of passion for different activities. I have a high degree of passion for team sports, movies, ancient

---

[61] This worked all the time in the beginning. It wasn't until I got older that I was able to tune him out effectively.

cultures, comedy, mental models, and psychology. I have a low degree of passion for swimming, cycling, sports with judges, cars, homework, finance, modern militaries, etc. A new book on Ancient Greece or social psychology? I'm in. A new book on cars or World War II? Pass.

If you truly have no interest whatsoever for an activity, then you shouldn't do it. Life is too short. If you just had an epiphany that you don't want to run anymore, I give you permission to stop. Find something you can truly engage in and dedicate yourself to that.

If you are even semi-passionate about running, then nurture that spark and give yourself a chance. Engage. Give that spark some fuel.

From Concentration to...What Were We Talking About?

Compared to most sports, a running workout is short. It's common for us to spend no more than one hour actually running. It's critical that we arrive mentally fresh, ready to concentrate on the task at hand and execute to the best of our ability.

But that requires us to have our minds in order first. If we have a bunch of things weighing on our minds, it is harder to truly focus on the workout.

This is easier said than done. We live in quite possibly the most distractive time in history. Is it just coincidence that the initials of Facebook, Instagram, Snapchat, and Twitter make the word FIST, given the way they are pounding us with non-stop distraction?[62] Add to that smartphones, flash sales, sports scores, podcasts, 24/7 news updates, streaming television, video games...there is always something to read, keep up with, or respond to.

There is a direct link between being connected and distracted. Concentrating takes effort, and concentrating in spite of distractions takes even more effort. Any extra effort you are spending on distractions is coming at the expense of your training.

---

[62] Yes, it's coincidence, but what a great acronym for my point!

Concentration is a necessary component to getting the most out of your workouts. Removing distractions is a great way to improve your ability to concentrate.

Measuring "What We Think About Most of the Time"

Degree of Focus

		Distraction	Concentration
	Passion	Mistakes	Purposeful
Degree of Interest			
	Disinterest	Poor Behavior	Faking It

Fig 38 - "What We Think About Most of the Time" determines how we act most of the time

When we combine Passion and Concentration we get the **"What-We-Think-About-Most-of-the-Time" Scale.** When our passion and our concentration are both high, we train purposefully. Maintaining this for one day ensures we have a great workout. Maintaining this for one season leads us to make a leap. Maintaining this for a career leads us to achieve our potential.

When we have a high passion but low concentration we make **Mistakes.** We fail to translate our positive energy into productivity. At the micro level, this could mean running a little too fast or too slow in an interval, or not stretching as well as we should.

More often than not, the mistake is so general we don't even see it. It is failing to get enough sleep because we get caught up doing something trivial. It is eating poorly because we didn't prepare something healthier. It is allowing ourselves to be distracted into a lifestyle that slows down our momentum.

There is a high probability the above paragraph hits home for you. That's good. Concentration is a habit you can develop, and we all have room for improvement.

Athletes with low passion and high concentration are what I affectionately call **Fakers**. And let me be clear: it's not always a bad thing to fake it. Life is filled with situations that we have to deal with despite our complete disinterest. It's better to fake it and get the most out of them.

With that said, Fakers never make the leap because they don't sustain the necessary quality work. They simply do enough to get by. If you are faking it, it's time to re-kindle your passion or move on.

There's not much to say about people with low passion and concentration. They will fail. If you find yourself on a team with someone in this mindset, you need to find a motivator that can shake them out of their disinterest. Any change will start with them caring.

Building habits of thought to create habits of behavior

Companies are always trying to automate expensive and manual processes. If they can agree on one best way to do it, they can save time and money.

We can take the same approach to save time and energy. The following are activities that help to change the way you think. We'll get into building physical habits in more detail in Chapter 9.

Make a Public Commitment: Our brains are hard-wired to seek consistency. We want to act based on our beliefs. The formal name for this is Consistency Bias and it is incredibly helpful to understand it. If we say we will do something, it actually pains us to not do it.

We can use this in our favor. By making a public commitment you will trigger deep-rooted mental processes that will ensure you live up to that commitment. And the more you state the commitment, the more you will compel yourself to stay consistent with it.

Next time you are talking with your coach, state the following: *"Getting the best out of myself is a top priority. I'll do the best I can to achieve it."*[63]

It will work. From that point on, your subconscious will push you to make decisions consistent with that statement. Everything else will start to fall in line.

> *"Say it to your coach: 'Getting the best out of myself is a top priority. I'll do the best I can to achieve it.'"*

Tomorrow's Key Three: Take 10 minutes each evening to think about the following day. Look at your calendar, the weather forecast, your to-do list, etc. Write down three things you want to execute optimally. Then write how you plan to do it.

For this to be effective, these should be effort-based objectives. For example, a good objective would be to execute your race plan. A bad objective (for this exercise) would be to win the race. The goal of the exercise is not to achieve success, but to think about the conditions necessary and align your activities accordingly.

Just writing down the "key three" will put you a big step closer to accomplishing them. But if you are really serious, find a teammate or coach or friend and swap "key threes" with them. Then, don't just send the new "key threes" for tomorrow, but also share whether or not you accomplished the three for today.

If three is too many, start with one. If every day is too frequent, do it once a week. But hold each other accountable. It is terrifying but transformative.

Digital Cleanse: The statistics on how often we look at our phones is alarming. The tradeoff of having the most powerful

---

[63] If you are a coach, you can ask your athletes the same question: Is getting the best out of yourself a top priority for you? Are you doing your best to achieve it?

and utilitarian technology ever invented in our pockets is that we can't stop using it.

The best way to regain control is to start with a two-week cleanse. You can do this in many levels:

- **Light Cleanse**: Find the one app that is sucking away the majority of your time and delete it. (You can always put it back on your phone in two weeks.) For me this was Facebook. For you it might be Instagram, Snapchat, or perhaps a game like Candy Crush. By deleting it, you force yourself to break a habit, which will trigger new decisions. Use the opportunity to choose something more productive.

- **Medium Cleanse**: Remove all the social and game apps from your phone. Every last one. This will eliminate the tendency to use your phone in all those small windows of time (waiting in line, waiting for your food to arrive, etc). Use that time to think about whatever aspect of your training/lifestyle you are trying to improve.

- **Deep Cleanse:** Put your phone on airplane mode and leave it in your bag when you go out. Turn off all notifications. Refuse to look at it wherever possible. When you get home, don't take it out to charge it (the battery should hardly be drained anyway). Challenge yourself to not look at it unless you have a specific reason, something you can't do without it.

Even a light digital cleanse will probably bother you for a bit. But you will also come to see that the time you are spending has low value, despite how engaging it is. It is rarely worth the distraction.

After two weeks, decide how much you want to let these apps/devices back into your life. Then make a set of rules that aligns with your ideal behavior. Make a public commitment to using your phone in your ideal way.

Tidy up: I remember reading the back of Marie Kondo's best-selling book *The Life-Changing Magic of Tidying* and being skeptical that organizing my things will make me "feel more confident, become more successful and be motivated to create the life you want."

I was wrong. It did just that.

Kondo's argument is relatively simple: We should only keep things in our lives that bring us joy; and we should take care to organize those things appropriately. She then systematically explains how and why to organize each type of item cluttering up your life.

Here's the interesting thing about this process. The first and largest part of the book is deciding what to keep and what to throw away. And while this sounds daunting, it actually becomes liberating. It forces you to practice decision-making.

Every decision to discard something is a decision that reinforces your priorities. There are things worth caring about and there are things that aren't. It gives you opportunities to say no, this is not good enough, I want better.

After you've said no to a hundred little things—the books or papers or knick-knacks that don't truly bring you any joy—you find it suddenly easier to say no to all the other things you are doing that may not bring you joy. I stopped going on Facebook, declined non-critical business meetings I didn't want to attend, changed frustrating daily routines, and quit my job to go live in Italy for a couple years.

Disorder is the result of decision-making and the habits that form around it. Changing the way you make decisions about the objects in your life will change the way you make decisions about everything else, including your training.

Final Thoughts on Causation

I'm pretty sure it was Bob Larsen who said that it takes three weeks to create a habit, and three days to lose it. It's a useful rule of thumb[64] for when you are trying to create new behaviors. It's not going to "just happen." You have to actively consider the new

---

[64] I lied. That was the third rule of thumb. You got me.

behaviors until they start to feel natural. And that can take a lot of time and effort.

You may have noticed that we didn't talk about goals. That may seem strange when the principle states "We become what we think about most of the time." Shouldn't we be thinking about our goals?

Well, yes and no.

But that's the topic for the next chapter.

Key Takeaways

1. All of your training activities should be considered to ensure they are effective and being executed efficiently. The goal is to consider them until we can do them without thinking about them.

2. The combination of passion and concentration determines how well we execute our behaviors. We should aim to pursue activities where we can maintain a high degree of both.

3. To create effective habits of behavior, we need to first create effective habits of thought.

PART II: Effort and Behavior

Chapter 8: Purpose
- *OTP #7: Optimal training is centered on clear, executable goals. We train to improve specific abilities.*
- What is Purposeful Practice?
- What Makes a Good Next Step Goal?
- Focus, Feedback and Comfort Zones
- Goals are Worthless but Goal-setting is Everything
- Five Goal-setting Strategies
- Goal Communication and Commitment

Spotlight: Next Level 80/20

Chapter 9: Discipline
- *OTP #8: Certain behaviors, if practiced with consistent quality, ensure Optimal Training.*
- The "Discipline = Willpower" Fallacy
- Discipline via Systems
- Creating a System
- The Many Benefits of Systems
- Simple Systems Everyone Needs
- Discipline, Systems, and Making a Leap

Chapter 10: Mistakes
- *OTP #9: Making mistakes is an effective way to learn and improve.*
- Mistakes of Commission vs Omission
- Four Types of Mistakes
- Risk and Performance Rewards
- Mistakes Sustain Momentum

Chapter 11: Analysis
- *OTP #10: Racing times and personal records indicate progress at one point in time.*
- Keep a Daily Activity Log
- Monthly Momentum Model
- Improving Our Analysis Generally
- "Respect your Position while Preparing for your Promotion"

Chapter 12: Perseverance
- *OTP #11: Optimal performances and realizing your potential are results of painstaking preparation and hard work.*
- Building Momentum Today = Think Big
- Sustaining Momentum Tomorrow = Think Small & Think All
- On Injuries And Other Predictable Obstacles
- Just Keep Rolling

Conclusion

8: Purpose: Make Every Workout Purposeful

In the first chapter, we learned about Jon Rankin's amazing leap. He attributed that leap to a change in how he set goals. Namely, he scrapped all the big future goals that had previously driven him—world records and national championships—and put all his effort into executing and enjoying his training.

There are two types of goals: motivational and executional. I think of motivational goals as "North Star" goals. They point us at a future destination, and guide us to stay on whatever path leads us there.

North Star goals have a few common characteristics. The objective is in the future. The goal is "result-based." And there are numerous obstacles (known and unknown) between our position today and achieving these goals in the future. The Momentum Model diagram assumes a North Star goal.

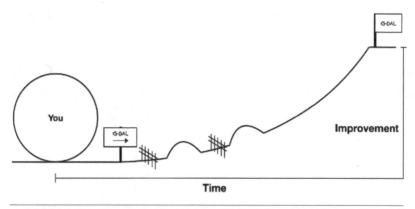

Fig 39 - The Momentum Model, in case you forgot.

Somehow, the word "goal" has come to mean North Star goals. It starts when we are little ("What do you want to be when you grow up?") and continues all throughout adulthood ("Where do you see yourself in five years?").

North Star goals are what Jon gave up. But he didn't eliminate goals from his training. He simply switched to execution goals, or what I call "Next Step" goals, which are the focus of this chapter.

OTP #7: Optimal training is centered on clear, executable goals. We train to improve specific abilities.

From a day-to-day training perspective, North Star goals are largely useless. Wanting to be a world champion or break a record doesn't help us get out of "stuck at our current level." But "stuck at our current level" is exactly what we need to focus on.

It's good to have an idea where you're going, and how you plan to get there. But in terms of our actual training sessions, Next Step goals are the only ones that matter.

Next Step goals aren't about the future, but the present.

Next Step goals aren't about getting there, but following the best route.

Next Step goals aren't about aspiration, but concentration.

If we are to put both goals in our Momentum Model, the North Star goals are the flag at the top of the hill. The thing we are striving to achieve before the end of the season, our graduation, or the end of our career.

Next Step goals are the outline of the arrows representing our effort in today's workout. They are outlines because our actual effort fills them in. Therefore, our Next Step goals represent how we *intend* to move forward. They are the quality of the push.

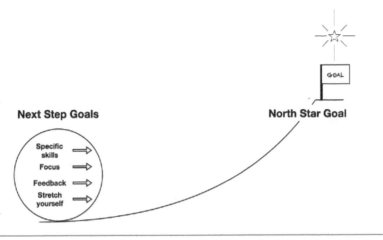

Fig 40 · Next Step goals push the ball forward today. North Star goals are where you hope to arrive.

A North Star goal gives us an idea of where we want to be. But it doesn't dictate the path to get there or what we need to do now to make progress. It stays out on the horizon, visible only when we look up from our work.

Next Step goals directly affect our momentum, which in turn determines whether or not we make a leap. They make up the core of Purposeful Practice, which is how we need to train to maximize our abilities.

Of all the positive internal behaviors driving us forward, Purposeful Practice is the most important.

What Is Purposeful Practice?

As you recall from the last chapter, athletes with better mental representations tend to perform better. How do they create better mental representations? By practicing purposefully.

Anders Ericsson, the researcher who coined the term 'mental representation,' identifies three types of practice.

Naive practice is "essentially just doing something repeatedly, and expecting that the repetition alone will improve one's performance." Naive practice includes just running every day, or just finishing each day's workout. Naive practice looks at a workout as a box to be checked, with the assumption that more checked boxes equals more improvement.

Purposeful Practice requires that every workout have a clear purpose: to improve specific abilities. We choose these abilities because they serve as stepping stones toward mastery.

	Goals	Focus	Feedback	Comfort
Purposeful Practice	Well-defined, Specific	Intense, Sustained	Immediate, Specific	Outside comfort zone
Naive Practice	Undefined, General	Mild, Sporadic	Delayed, Generic	Inside comfort zone

Fig 41 - Purposeful Practice is a much more effective approach to training than Naive Practice

In a running context, the abilities we seek to improve are our endurance, speed, strength, flexibility, coordination, form, sense of pace, concentration, reaction time, recovery, self-efficacy and competitiveness (among others).

We use different training methods to improve these abilities: long runs, intervals, fartlek, tempo runs, recovery runs, cross-training, weight training, stretching, visualization, planning, analysis, etc.

Nobody goes directly from a beginner to an expert. We have to master our current level before we can jump to the next. We need to create the mental representations and physical abilities to execute effectively.

There are four main components of Purposeful Practice:
1. Well-defined, specific execution goals ("Next Step" goals)
2. Focus

3. Immediate feedback
4. Getting out of our comfort zone

When you practice purposefully you don't just do a workout. You use the workout to improve specific abilities. You focus intensely throughout, receive and act on constructive feedback, and–physically or mentally–push yourself out of your comfort zone.

There are two things worth pointing out. First, you can have a sophisticated training program and still approach it naively. It is Naive Practice when you focus only on finishing the workout. I trained under Bob Larsen–one of the greatest coaches ever–for my first three years at UCLA, but I approached the workouts with a Naive Practice mindset for much of that time.

Second, Purposeful Practice as described by Ericsson is not the highest level of practice possible. He identifies an even higher level of practice called Deliberate Practice.

Deliberate Practice is Purposeful Practice with elite coaching. It is only possible when success can be measured clearly and best practices for coaching are well-defined.

Obviously, this applies to distance running. So why do I advocate Purposeful Practice and not Deliberate Practice?

The only difference between the two is access to the best coaching.

Our objective is for you to make a leap. You don't need a new coach to do that. Purposeful Practice will be enough.

If you can get access to world class coaching, do it! When you do, your Purposeful Practice will become Deliberate Practice. Until that time, a lack of access to world class coaching is no excuse.

What Makes a Good Next Step Goal?

Purposeful practice requires us to have clear and achievable Next Step goals. So what makes a good Next Step goal?
1. It is achievable today, at this practice, in this moment
2. It connects to the larger training program

3. It requires intense focus and concentration
4. It creates or enhances our mental representation for a specific ability

No matter what type of workout you are doing, there are ways to focus on doing it better. If you are doing hard 800 meter repeats, the Next Step goal will be part of the answer to the question: what would a "perfect 800 meter repeats workout" look like?

We can break down an 800 meter repeats workout into a few specific abilities: to hit our splits and interval times; to maintain our form as we get fatigued; to respond to others' movements on the track; to feel the pace and adjust accordingly; to recognize the onset of lactic acid buildup and respond accordingly.

We may not focus on all of these in one workout. It's fine to pick one and focus on that. But if your workout does not require you to maintain your focus and concentration throughout then you haven't set an effective Next Step goal.

The difference between an expert and a beginner is not the ability to complete the workout. It's the ability to *get the most out of the workout*. This comes from experience and engagement.

> *"The difference between an expert and a beginner isn't the ability to complete the workout. It's the ability to get the most out of it."*

If you are a beginner, your mental representation of an interval workout will be less defined. Your focus will be to simply finish the workout. This is normal, but it's not good enough. You are still responsible for knowing the workout's purpose and doing your best to achieve it.

As you gain more experience, you will begin to see how each workout can be used to refine different abilities. The combination of pace, rest and quantity will dictate how far outside your comfort zone you will be pushed and how much you will need to focus.

But what should our Next Step goal be for all the road runs and long runs we put in around those hyper-focused interval workouts? Ericsson gives an example from the Olympic swimmer Natalie Coughlin, who realized she could use all those hours of training to identify what the perfect swimming stroke should feel like.

By focusing intensely on this one aspect during all of her endurance work, she took "naive practice" time and made it purposeful. It also led to her first leap, and she credits it with being the key to all of her success.

Absent another specific goal to focus on, use your "road run" time to focus on your form, your stride and your breathing. The goal: understand your body and how it feels at the pace you are running. This will lead to the longer-term goal of developing a habit of intense focus.

Focus, Feedback and Comfort Zones

We've covered how focus is integrally tied to our Next Step goals. Maintaining concentration throughout a workout is as important as the physical improvements we make in our training. Some of us are naturally better at it, but we can all develop the ability. Unfortunately, many athletes don't realize it's a skill they need to develop.

Getting feedback on our performance is also critical, and the more immediate the better. Feedback comes in all shapes and sizes. Knowing your splits to help maintain your pace, catching a slip in concentration, or being called out for not being prepared in the first place.

The quality of your feedback determines the quality of your execution. You should know what feedback to expect from your coach, and what you are expected to generate yourself (how you feel mid-interval, your heart rate post interval, etc). The more your feedback is constructive and aligned to your training goals, the more it will help you improve.

"The quality of your feedback determines the quality of your execution."

My first collegiate 1500 meter race was a night meet at Occidental College in Pasadena, California. Everyone loved Occidental because it was a "fast track." Everyone ran personal bests there.

I had at least seven teammates in my race. My personal best of 4:05 was run two years prior in high school, and I wanted to beat that time. For the first three laps I zoned out with the Lenny Kravitz song "I just wanna flyyyyy awayyyyy" playing in my head. (Why I remember that detail I have no idea.)

Suddenly, amidst the shouting and cheering and bell-ringing I heard Coach Larsen. He said just five words, calmly and casually, but with a hint of impatience: "Get in the race, Green."

Dzzzt. Lenny went silent. The race was almost over! I found another gear and surprised everyone by finishing 3rd in a new personal best of 3:55. That time surprised me and changed what I thought was possible that season. I'm not sure I would have run as well that year if I'd run 4:02, for example.

What sticks with me now isn't the time or the fast track or Lenny, but my loss of focus and the timeliness of my coach's feedback. Those five words might have altered my entire career.

Lastly, we need get out of our comfort zone. We can do this a few ways:

- We can increase the intensity beyond what we are used to
- We can increase quantity (mileage, number of reps), or
- We can try to do something new

It is worth repeating. There is no point in increasing intensity or quantity until you are executing at 100% at your current level. Quality sustains momentum and leads to making a leap.

So I recommend you get out of your comfort zone by trying something new.

Challenge yourself to improve your focus and concentration throughout each workout. Practice getting locked in. Know what your Next Step goals are and focus relentlessly on them. Not just in your interval workouts, but in your recovery runs as well.

There's no problem with having a nice run with your teammates and enjoying the conversation. But take some recovery runs on your own and challenge yourself to focus on the run, to stay as relaxed as possible, to feel every stride.

You do not need to get *physically* outside your comfort zone in every workout. A well-designed training program has many maintenance and recovery activities. Use them to focus on your mental game.

Goals are Worthless but Goal-setting is Everything.

Generally speaking, it's important to be motivated and North Star goals can be a good source of motivation. But just like a Coke can be a refreshing drink on a hot day, it's still empty calories. North Star goals are the empty calories of achievement.

I don't expect you to agree with me. The importance of North Star goals has been drilled into all of us, with various methodologies and techniques for getting the most out of them: WOOP,[65] SMART,[66] BHAG,[67] etc. I know you'll keep setting them, in part because everybody will expect you to.

But let me give you a simple scenario. Imagine you are a 4:15 miler in high school. You can choose a North Star goal of "being a sub-4 miler" or "winning the Olympic gold medal." Which one is better?

It's a trick question. Neither one is better! If they motivate you to get out the door and do the work, then either is fine.

---

[65] Wish, Outcome, Obstacle, Plan. This methodology gets one thing right: acknowledging obstacles and how to overcome them.

[66] Specific, Measurable, Achievable, Realistic, Time-related. Under this methodology, goals must adhere to the above five criteria.

[67] Big Hairy Audacious Goal. Mostly used in business, by people who like to use business-y words.

It doesn't matter that one is based on time and the other position. Nor that one is a significantly higher level than the other.[68] Nor that one is more realistic than the other. The specifics just don't matter.

I shared this quote earlier: "Plans are worthless but planning is everything."

The same is true for goals. The goals themselves are worthless. Goal-setting is everything.

> ## "Goals are worthless, but goal-setting is everything."

Five Goal-Setting Strategies

Do a value check: Instead of imagining yourself on the podium, imagine the work it will take to get there and the lifestyle you will need to maintain. If you aren't sure, take whoever is closest to that level now and substitute their training program and lifestyle as a proxy. If you lived and trained like that person, would you feel fulfilled?

There's a romanticism that creeps in when we think about achieving long-term goals. We imagine the benefits in detail and we disregard the costs. Whether you aspire to be an Olympic champ, an entrepreneur, a Kardashian or a thought-leader, living the life is less sexy than it appears on Instagram.

A North Star goal must align to who you are as a person. If you can't imagine being the Future You that your goal requires, you have a big problem. As my friend Jon Rankin says, "You need to be the person before you become the person."

The order of events is not 1) achieve greatness, then 2) change lifestyle to sustain it. *Excellence is a result of your lifestyle.*

---

[68] You need to be able to run a 3:47 mile to be competitive for the gold medal in most years.

The order is 1) change lifestyle and training quality, then 2) achieve greatness. In the time between 1 and 2, you need to do the work without the payoff.

Obstacles over Arrivals: Part of the joy of setting a North Star goal is imagining how great it will be when you achieve it.

Scrap that. Focusing on the arrival is what will *keep you from* achieving it.

The true value in having a North Star goal is in how you plan to achieve it. And planning is primarily about identifying obstacles. Who will you live with? How will you pay the bills? How will you increase your mileage without getting injured? How will you maintain your motivation when you hit a big obstacle?

The more obstacles you identify, the more plans you can make. All of those plans will probably be useless, but the act of making them will lead you to make better decisions. And besides, avoiding obstacles is a great way to maintain momentum.[69]

Backcasting: Backcasting means to forecast backward. Start at your North Star goal and try to figure out exactly what it will take to get there.

To win the gold medal you will need to improve by X seconds in Y time. You will need to develop the best stamina and/or finishing kick in the world. You will need to be comfortable running in high-pressure situations. You will need to stay injury free, and improve your positive feedback loops over a long time.

Backcasting shows exactly what is required. You can identify areas where you are making big assumptions. If you find yourself saying, "I'll run 100-plus miles per week for the next three years"–but you've never successfully maintained over 70 without getting injured–then you have a disconnect.

If you can't tell a plausible story in which you navigate all the obstacles on the path to your goal, then you need to change the goal or keep working on the plan.

---

[69] How is this different from WOOP? I don't consider the Wish and Outcome portion of WOOP to be relevant. You can pick literally anything that requires you to improve and the result will be the same. The only part that matters is the OP: Obstacles and Planning.

Pre-Mortem: Here's a twist on the last one. A post-mortem is an analysis of why someone or something died. A pre-mortem is a hypothetical analysis of why a plan doesn't work out.

Here's how it works: Set your big North Star goal. Now tell the most likely story you can imagine for why you failed to achieve it. Then imagine other scenarios or combinations of factors that could cause you to fail.

The more versions of this story you can tell, the more obstacles you will identify. If you are going to keep this North Star goal, then you need plans for making sure none of your make believe pre-mortems become a real life post-mortem.

Unfix your timeframe: Fixing the time for your North Star goal doesn't add a lot of value. The only practical way to set a time goal is to draw a linear line, but improvement isn't linear. So don't bother pretending.

Use time as a variable to compare situations. Achieving a goal in one year might require a more aggressive training program than achieving the same goal in three years. Comparing the two options can be useful. Don't just arbitrarily choose one.

As for situations like the Olympics, which happen on a fixed schedule, focus on putting yourself in the best position to first make the team, then compete when you are there. It's a subtle difference, but by shifting from a norm-referenced goal (make the team, win a medal) to a self-referenced goal (put myself in the best position to be there/win it) you will emphasize the work that will get you there.

Again, the goal itself doesn't matter. If setting a North Star goal illuminates obstacles, reasons for failure, and your core values, then it might make a difference. Or to rephrase Eisenhower's insight on planning:

Goals are worthless but goal-setting is everything.

Goal Communication and Commitment

Next Step goals and North Star goals both have one important aspect in common. They become more achievable when they are concrete.

Having a goal in mind can be useful. Writing a goal on a piece of paper is better because *it is more concrete*. Telling others about your goal is the best because *it becomes a commitment*.

"Telling others about your goals turns them into a commitment."

Committing to our goals aligns our positive arrows in the right direction. For Next Step goals, it helps us get critical feedback, catch slips in concentration, and get support as we leave our comfort zone. These are essential to Purposeful Practice and building strong mental representations.

For North Star goals, commitment helps us stay engaged, be held accountable, and maintain our positive habits and systems. This is especially useful for dealing with obstacles. Stating clearly what obstacles you are worried about both commits you to prepare for them and gives others the opportunity to assist you.

Communicate your goals. You will be more likely to achieve them.

Key Takeaways

1. There are two main types of goals, executional and motivational. Next Step goals are things we focus on in the moment. North Star goals are outcomes we hope to achieve in the future.

2. Purposeful practice is the key to maximizing your training. Clear execution goals are essential to purposeful practice, as

are intense focus, immediate feedback and going outside our comfort zone.

3. North Star goals are primarily useful as drivers of motivation. We maximize their value when we align them with our core values, identify potential obstacles, and plan for all the ways we might not achieve them.

Spotlight: Next Level 80/20

O ur last spotlight introduced the 80/20 Rule. This one takes it to the next level. Literally.

Question: what if we applied the 80/20 rule to itself?

Next Level 80/20

We can think of the 80/20 Rule as being Level 1. In Level 1 we take all our training activities and identify the 20% that drive the majority of our results.

But surely within that initial 20% the activities are not all equal. What happens when we reapply the 80/20 Rule to that top 20%? What is the top 20% of our top 20%?

I call this Next Level 80/20, and it looks like this:

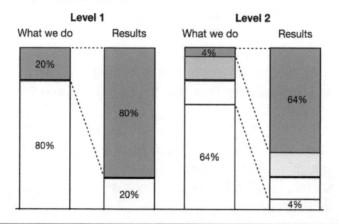

Fig 42 - Next Level 80/20 takes our most important activities and applies the 80/20 Rule to them

The top 20% of our top 20% is 4%. The top 80% of our 80% is 64%.

What does this tell us? That nearly two-thirds of our success is driven by just 4% of our efforts! It also tells us that up to two-thirds of our daily activities result in just 4% of our total success.

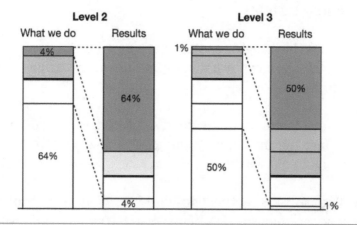

Fig 43 - Next Level 80/20 tells us that 1% of our activities could lead to 50% of our success or failure

How about the next level after that? Then we find that 1% of our input accounts for 50% of our results. The other 99%–the vast vast majority of what we do–leads to the remaining 50%.

If you're like most people you're feeling a bit skeptical right now. Am I seriously arguing that 1% of what we do results in 50% of our results?

Actually, YES. Here's a simple example. 1% of our day is about 15 minutes. If you spend 15 minutes prioritizing your day and creating a good plan, you can definitely increase your results by up to 50%. That 15 minutes can improve your output in every other area of your day.

But again, don't be concerned with the numbers. This is a mental model. It's a way of thinking.

We train better when we assume that a small number of our activities generate the majority of our results, and we maximize our effort in those areas.

Whether 1% of what we do drives 50% or 30% or 70% of our success, it doesn't change what we need to do. We need to nail that 1%.

Three Key Insights

1. 80/20 thinking doesn't stop at Level 1. Once you've identified Level 1, you can use the 80/20 rule on that group of activities, too.

2. There is one "Most Effective" activity: We can't put our energy into the most important activity unless we've taken the time to figure out what it is.

3. The "Most Effective" activity is enormously important: It may not account for 50% of our results, but it could. It will definitely have a 10x return compared to most other activities.

What is the Next Level 80/20 of Training?

The goal of every athlete's training program is to create positive feedback loops, gain and sustain massive momentum, and make a leap.

To that end we must ask the following: what is the 20% of our training that most contributes to positive feedback loops and making a leap?

Level 1 (Top 20%): Have an optimal training mindset. Approach every workout with the right mindset and attitudes. Engage in your training. Take responsibility. View everything through the lens of your effort and preparation. Build up your self-efficacy and develop strong mental habits.

Practically, this means doing what you need to do to feel good at the start of every workout. Eat well, hydrate, rest, recover. Understand the hidden curriculum and identify 80/20 activities. Maximize the ones that drive the most improvement, and minimize the ones that don't.

Within these activities, what is the Next Level 80/20?

Level 2 (Top 4%): Practice Purposefully. Know what specific skills you are aiming to improve and what a high quality workout looks like. Set clear Next Step goals and stay hyper-focused on achieving them. Build better feedback into your training by asking better questions. Get out of your comfort zone, both physically and mentally.

The more you understand what a great workout looks like, the more you'll be able to do them.

Within this approach, is there another Next Level 80/20? I think so.

Level 3 (Top 1%): Do the work. For distance runners, this means running long, hard runs that maximize your aerobic threshold. Runners need to run hard. You're at least 50% of your way to success just by lacing up your shoes and hitting the roads hard day after day. This consistent effort is the core positive force driving your momentum forward.

Rest-of-80%: Keep it positive. What about all the other stuff in your life, the people you spend time with and the hobbies you pursue? The effects of these activities are smaller, but if enough of them are negative they will slow your momentum and keep you from making a leap.

Use Next Level 80/20 thinking to figure out which of these are providing the least value and minimize how much time and energy you spend on them. We often have one person or one activity or one belief that holds us back more than all the rest. Find it and fix it.

9. Discipline: Systematically Eliminating the Unproductive

Our formal training program takes up roughly 20% of our time. It is the 20% of our day that accounts for 80% of our results. Purposeful Practice maximizes that time.

The remaining 80%–all the activities that make up the Hidden Training Program–accounts for just 20% of our results. This last 20% can't be ignored.

Being 80% successful gets us nowhere. A feedback loop that is 80% positive will not result in a large leap. We need to optimize our lives outside of practice, too. But we need to do it thoughtfully, so we conserve our mental energy for Purposeful Practice.

In this chapter we will dig into the Hidden Training Program, understand how to simplify and systematize it, and make this time work for us.

OTP #8: Certain behaviors, if practiced with consistent quality, ensure Optimal Training.

Many athletes live undisciplined, unfocused lives that undermine their hard work. Their lifestyles hold them back. One clear sign an athlete will make a leap is a significant improvement in how they spend their time *outside of practice*. Improvements here don't just increase momentum. They are an indication that the athlete is overcoming the "discipline illusion."

The Discipline Illusion is the belief that maintaining a disciplined lifestyle is restrictive and exhausting. It's restrictive because it requires too many sacrifices and limits our freedom. It's exhausting because it requires too many decisions and too much willpower.

	Decisions	Restrictions	Willpower
Discipline Illusion	Too many	Too many No freedom No fun	Too much Exhausting
Actual Experience	Fewer Well-considered	Few Low priority items	Less Conserved for practice

Fig 44 - The Discipline Illusion makes people think discipline is more exhausting than it is

The funny thing is, disciplined people don't feel this way. Their lifestyle doesn't restrict them because they aren't sacrificing anything important. They haven't given up freedom. They've focused on their priorities.

And they aren't exhausted at all. Rather, what exhausts them is being undisciplined! They know discipline isn't the result of lots of decisions and enormous willpower. It is the result of a few carefully considered decisions, some thoughtful routines, and an environment that makes it easy.

Seeing through the Discipline Illusion starts with understanding one critical point. Discipline is not willpower.

The "Discipline = Willpower" Fallacy

Disciplined people aren't working any harder than undisciplined people. In fact, they often use *less* willpower and make *fewer* decisions.

> *"Disciplined people often use **less** willpower and make **fewer** decisions."*

They do this by satisfying two conditions:
1. They make discipline their "lazy default"
2. They create a "disciplined" environment

Make discipline the lazy default.

Our "lazy default" is what we do when we don't want to put energy into something. We do our lazy default when we are tired, distracted, or simply can't be bothered. Often, it's how we approach all the activities we don't like or don't understand well. Things like cooking, cleaning, managing finances, or talking to those weird neighbors who always seem to be in the elevator.

We do our "lazy default" because it's acceptable, routine, and easy. Not just one, but all three.

Acceptable: An activity is acceptable if it aligns to the rules we live by.

This assumes, of course, that you have rules you live by. If you don't, you should.

Rules simplify decision-making, especially around impulsive behaviors. They create a pre-decision, which means you don't have to analyze the situation and weigh costs and benefits...you just need to follow your rule. They also enhance our sense of commitment, which can offset any feeling of sacrifice.

But rules only work when they align to our priorities and purpose. If the rule has no obvious connection to how you want to live, you won't follow it consistently.

A couple years ago I made a rule that I don't drink soda. This wasn't easy for me. I love soda. There's nothing better than a 72-ounce Dr. Pepper to get you through the LA traffic.[70] But few things are worse for us. Cutting out soda was an 80/20 decision for improving my diet. I thought about it, made the rule, and created routines around drinking more water and tea.[71]

A well-considered rule allows you to make a decision once about what is and is not acceptable. Following it becomes both effective and efficient.

Routine: Rules help to determine what you do, but they aren't enough. We need to turn our rules into routines.

Training routines aren't complicated. Take sit-ups. A strong core is essential to your ability to breathe, but doing sit-ups kinda sucks. You don't want to be deciding every day when to do them and what kind of sit-ups you will do. That was my initial approach, and I frequently put them off until just before bedtime, when I either decided not to do them or did a few quick sets and then lay in bed waiting for my heart rate to come down so I could sleep.

My first change was a rule: every run must end with sit-ups. Whether a morning jog or an afternoon interval workout, I wasn't done until I'd done sit-ups.

Then I made a routine. The actual sit-ups involved seven different positions, to isolate different muscle groups. One minute spent on each position, seven minutes total. Since I often ran twice per day, I got about 15 minutes of core work in each day, at the ideal time to get it done.

We eventually made it a team routine, and we all did core work together after workouts. We mixed up the order of the po-

---

[70] My nominee for this year's "most American sentence" award.

[71] Another bonus to having rules: Rules also help you avoid or get out of situations you don't want to be in. If someone is pushing you to be undisciplined, one of the best ways to get out it is to simply say, "I have a rule."

It doesn't matter if they agree with your rule. People naturally respect consistency and commitment, and are more likely to respect your decision.

sitions to add variety, but knowing we were doing all seven kept it routine. The result: I increased my core strength without adding to my mental workload.

Make sure all your routines are "previously considered." If you have ineffective routines, you will still do them. We do our lazy default.

> ## "If you have ineffective routines, you will still do them. We do our lazy default."

Easy: When we have effective rules and routines, the work is 90% done. But we can still get stuck if it isn't easy. Doing one thousand sit-ups is never "easy." But doing it via a routine is "easier" and that makes us more likely to be successful.

What we are most worried about here is mental effort, or "cognitive load." **Cognitive load** is the effort being used by our working memory. The more we actively consider what we are doing, the higher the cognitive load. Rules and routines decrease cognitive load.

So does improving your environment.

Create a "disciplined" environment.

Your environment is everything external: your team, school, work, family and friends, living space, and hobbies. But it can also include things as simple as your socks, a note on a wall or even a key chain.

Our environment is filled with behavioral triggers. A trigger is anything that initiates a thought or behavior. These triggers influence what we choose to do, how well we do it, and how we feel about it afterwards. Some triggers are positive, some are negative. Some are strong, some are weak.

If an environment triggers high quality, momentum generating thoughts and behaviors, we do them. If it triggers ineffective, momentum killing thoughts and behaviors, then we do those.

Disciplined people create an environment that triggers successful behaviors.

"Disciplined people create an environment that triggers successful behaviors."

Who you spend time with is the most important. Friends, family, coworkers, classmates and teammates either encourage your discipline or discourage it.

When a team consistently reinforces positive triggers, it is easy to do disciplined work. Not just during practice, but before and after as well.

When a team lacks discipline, athletes become undisciplined. It is possible to overcome this with willpower, but not forever. And if you use your willpower for this, you won't have it for purposeful practice.

If you are stuck on an undisciplined team, create a "discipline bubble." Find one other person and commit to staying disciplined together. Reinforce each other. Once your other teammates see your commitment, they will join you. And when they do, make sure you set the terms.

For others in your life, decide how positive they are and give them your time based on that metric. Surround yourself with people who make you better.

You can improve your physical environment as well. We drink more water when water is always with us. We stretch and do core exercises better when we have a dedicated space for these exercises. A simple reminder seen frequently can trigger us to behave in a certain way. Those WWJD bracelets really work.

I once had a professor give me a keychain with the letters "PCG" on it. The letters stood for "Personal Challenge to Greatness." This simple keychain was a positive trigger machine. I saw it when I left the house, when I drove my car, and when I got home and took the keys out of my pocket. I still have it 20 years later.[72]

I believe this so strongly that I've built a company around it. My company, Go Be More,[73] sells apparel to help you commit to your goals. By associating your goals to a physical object, you make them concrete and you improve your consistency. Every little boost helps.

Take control of your environment. Make the right behaviors not just easy, but inevitable. Create "lazy defaults" that keep your momentum strong without requiring extra mental energy.

When you do you will have more than just a routine. You will have a System.

Discipline via Systems

For our purposes, a "system" is anything you do regularly that sustains positive momentum. The best systems keep you going in the right direction with minimal effort.

Systems can be simple or complex. Simpler is better because it is easier to execute. Don't add complexity unless you are convinced it is worth it.

Brushing your teeth is a system. Some people keep it simpler than others:

- Brush every night
- Brush with an electric toothbrush every night
- Brush with an electric toothbrush morning and night
- Brush with an electric toothbrush using a timer and floss after every meal

Each of the above is a system. They all are routines based on rules we believe in and done in an environment that makes them easy to accomplish. All of them are momentum-positive, because they contribute to our health.

---

[72] I wrote about it on the Go Be More blog on 10/5/2019.

[73] https://gobemore.co

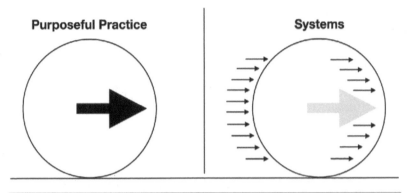

Purposeful Practice   **Systems**

Fig 45 - Purposeful Practice creates a massive positive arrow. Systems create many small ones.

You have a finite amount of willpower. You need to focus your willpower on Purposeful Practice. For everything else, create systems that streamline your life.

The more you can keep all the arrows from the Hidden Training Program pointing forward, the more likely you are to make a leap. Purposeful Practice will always drive the majority of your improvement, but you can't let the rest of your life act as a drag.

Creating a System

So how do we create a new system? Start with the following questions:

1. How central is this activity to your performance goals?
2. What is the minimum you need to do to keep your momentum going forward?
3. Can you create a rule you will consistently follow?
4. Can you tweak your environment to make it easier?

How central is the activity to your performance goals?

Person A wants to be a champion runner. Person B wants to be the mouth model for toothpaste commercials. Person A needs purposeful practice for running and a system for teeth care. Person B needs the opposite.

Your life is filled with important things that are not central to our performance goals: looking good, paying bills, enjoying hobbies. These are good candidates to be systems.

What is the minimum you need to do to keep your momentum going forward?

The goal of a system is consistent success with minimal effort. Start by identifying the *minimum required* to stay "momentum positive." This is your fall-back position. If you do more, that's great, but when all else fails you need to commit to doing at least this much.

It is fine to set your system at your minimum, but if you can get a bigger benefit for little extra effort, do more.

Can you create a rule you will consistently follow?

A good rule is something you personally agree with and everyone can understand (even if they don't agree). The best rules are absolute: "I brush my teeth every night." There is no ambiguity and they are easy to follow.

But new systems need a little slack. For new systems, start with a *pre-conditional rule*. This rule commits you to doing the preparation for the behavior you want. Let's say you want to create a system around studying. A pre-conditional rule might be: "I will sit at my desk for five minutes with my book open and phone turned off."

If you were just feeling a bit lazy, you will overcome it and start studying. If after five minutes you still don't feel like it, fine. You did your minimum. Don't beat yourself up over it. Even the most disciplined people need a break once in a while.[74]

---

[74] If you are constantly following your precondition rule but not doing the behavior you want, then your system doesn't work. Start over.

A good system defines your minimum. It doesn't guarantee success. It puts you in position to be successful.

Can you tweak your environment to make it easier?

Your environment includes where you are, who you are with, what you have with you, and anything that interrupts your attention.

Imagine your system is to do sit-ups after every run. Shouldn't you finish your runs where it's easy to do sit-ups? Can you lay out the yoga mat beforehand? What if you hung up a calendar with check marks for every time you did your sit-ups? Find ways to add triggers and remove friction.

Positive triggers plus clear rules plus no friction equals discipline by lazy default.

The Many Benefits of Systems

The main benefit of a system is that it keeps you progressing with little effort. But there are some other benefits worth mentioning.

Execution-oriented: Systems align with Next Step goals. We do them now, in the present.

Habit-forming: Systems create a habit of success. Good systems are either done or not done. There are no benchmarks, no plans, and no milestones. If you execute your system, you were 100% successful. It feels good to be successful.

Compounding: Systems align with exponential thinking. Slow and steady progress is critical to making a leap. A good system puts the emphasis on daily progress more than future results.

Self-referenced: Systems are self-referenced. They aren't about achieving; they are about maintaining. As your long-term goals become self-referenced, your systems will fit in perfectly.

Personal: You can create systems for your personal circumstances. When conditions aren't ideal, a system can help to create the feeling of success.

When I was at UCLA I planned a six-week trip to Europe with my teammate, Martin. I had a detailed summer training program but was doubtful I could execute it. Coach Peterson knew that if I tried to follow a regular training program, I would fail and add stress to my trip. I'd come back disappointed in my training, conflicted about my trip, and feeling like I'd lost momentum.

So we created a simple system: run at least 5 times a week for as much as makes sense.

This gave me a rule (5x/week), identified my minimum (as much as makes sense), created tons of flexibility, and allowed me to adapt based on the environment. Some days I ran three miles, others twelve. By sticking to this minimal system I felt successful, I stressed less, and I still came back in decent shape.[75]

Never discount the power of *feeling successful*. Effective systems create the repeated feeling of success.

> ## "Never discount the power of feeling successful."

Simple Systems Everyone Needs

There are several areas where you need a system. Or multiple smaller systems. There are entire books written about each of these so I will keep it brief. You're engaged, responsible, and thoughtful. You'll find what works for you.

---

[75] This was my summer training the season I made a leap.

Sleep: Outside of training, sleep is the most important aspect of your life for achieving optimal performance. It affects your physical recovery, your ability to focus, and your ability to process feedback. Bad sleep will destroy your training feedback loop. Some 80/20 ideas:

- Go to bed at the same time every night, no matter what.
- Invest in a good mattress and pillow. It's worth it.
- Eliminate TV or electronic gadgets for 30 minutes before bed.
- Sneak a nap into your schedule wherever possible.

Diet: You don't have to go crazy here. Just identify your biggest weaknesses and figure out simple ways to reduce or eliminate them. A lot of diet is availability, so be sure there is as little friction as possible around eating well. Some 80/20 ideas:

- Eat fruit for dessert.
- Skip appetizers. They are usually unhealthy and make you more likely to over-eat.
- Keep food you don't want to eat out of the house entirely. Make it a rule!
- Count your chews. It slows you down, improves digestion, and you appreciate the food more.
- Avoid buffets. If your school's dining hall is all-you-can-eat, make a rule that you can only eat what you get on the first pass.[76]

Hydration: Here's a rule of thumb.[77] If your mouth is dry or your pee is yellow, you need to drink more. If you're not sure whether you've been drinking enough water, drink more water. Some 80/20 ideas:

- Always have water with you. No excuses.
- Every time you drink water, take 10 sips.
- Save sports drinks for after workouts. They are super sugary so make them a treat rather than the norm.

---

[76] TBD if this will be a problem post-coronavirus!

[77] Oh dear, that's number four.

- Coffee and tea are not dehydrating, despite what you may have heard. Feel free to enjoy a glass or two, especially when it's cold outside.

Monitoring Progress: I think of this as keeping a training log, a daily diary, or any other system for keeping track of your work. Some 80/20 ideas:
- Use whatever tool you enjoy using. A leather-bound diary, an Excel spreadsheet or an app can all work.
- One hour reviews. Same time, same place, every week.
- Note anything unusual, funny or insightful that happened. It makes both writing and reviewing your logs more enjoyable.
- Share your training logs with someone: a coach, a teammate, a parent. It will boost accountability.

Learning and Engaging: Reading and thinking about training related topics increases engagement. Carve out that time. Focus on applying new ideas and insights to your personal experience. Some 80/20 ideas:
- Skim books to find the most interesting topics. Read those first. (Books follow the 80/20 rule, too.)
- Team book club. Get a teammate to read one book per week with you. Talk about it on your long run.
- Apply concepts to your training. Whatever you are learning about, consider how it might apply to running.

Hygiene / Chores / Maintenance: I'm sure you all have wonderful hygiene, spotless houses and everything in life is always running smoothly. But just in case that should change in the future... Some 80/20 ideas:
- Listen to podcasts while doing chores.
- Hire someone to do it. It's usually worth it.
- Buy pre-shrunk and wrinkle free.

Relaxation and Entertainment: It's easy to get sucked into unproductive activities. Some systems should focus on "not starting." Others need to focus on "stopping." Some 80/20 ideas:

- Delete apps. Just delete them. I've never found an app I couldn't re-install.
- Turn off notifications. Check for updates on your terms.
- Watch highlights of late night shows. You don't have to watch them in real time. All the funny will be there in the morning.

Family, Friends and Partners: It is so hard to be successful when your family, your friends or your partner are a net negative (in terms of your training). You don't need to cut them out entirely. You need to have a system for establishing the rules of your engagement. Some 80/20 ideas:

- Propose alternatives. If you don't want to go drinking, propose meeting for breakfast one morning.
- Set guidelines. "I'm happy to hang out but I don't want to do X..."
- Define what you need. Remember, it's your life.[78]
- A few friends provide the most value in your life. Keep in touch with them.

We didn't include activities like weight training, cross-training, medical treatment, and pre- and post-race routines. Those all fall under the umbrella of your training program. Approach them with a Purposeful Practice mindset. But if you think a system will help you, create one!

Discipline, Systems, and Making a Leap

We aren't seeking discipline at all costs. We are seeking discipline at reasonable costs. 80/20 discipline. At least to start.

---

[78] Similarly, find out what they need. If you aren't the best person to provide it, make that clear.

Systems are the best way to get 80/20 discipline. They are personal, immediate, progress-oriented, and—here's the best part—*lazy*. They allow us to do what we need to do without all the wasted mental energy.

When you combine Purposeful Practice with effective systems, you maintain your momentum. But there's still one thing that can hold you back: mistakes.

Key Takeaways

1. The Discipline Illusion causes undisciplined people to think discipline is restrictive and exhausting. In fact, discipline can lead to easier decision-making and less energy spent.

2. Discipline is not the product of willpower. It is the product of aligning our "lazy default" behaviors and removing environmental obstacles.

3. A system is a set of behaviors designed to keep your momentum moving forward with the minimal effort required.

4. Systems are best used for non-training activities that have a high probability of affecting our overall performance. These include sleep, diet, hydration and other day-to-day activities.

10. Mistakes: Strive To Make 'em Better

I t sucks to make mistakes. Especially when everyone is watching or our teammates are depending on us. In a perfect world we wouldn't make any mistakes, and we would spare ourselves the trauma, right?

In fact, the opposite is true. Mistakes are essential, invigorating, and educational. That is, if you think about them the right way. This chapter explores how to think about mistakes in our training, because they *will* happen.

OTP #9: Making mistakes is an effective way to learn and improve.

First things first, mistakes are always mental. Always. As we discussed in Chapter 7, all behavior is caused and all causation is mental.

What is a mistake? It is an accidental or ineffective behavior. Which means we can reduce them if we understand them.

Mistakes of Commission vs Omission

A **mistake of commission** occurs because of your direct action. You made a bad choice; you moved in the wrong way; you said the wrong thing; you tried to do something and weren't able to do it. These mistakes are the most obvious and easy to analyze. "I started out too fast." "I ate too much before my workout." "I told my partner she looks fat in that outfit."

You did it and because you take responsibility you need to analyze what led to that action and figure out how to correct it.

A **mistake of omission** occurs when you fail to act and get a sub-optimal result. It's when you wait and the opportunity passes, or you fail to try and don't achieve what you could have. "I didn't stretch enough." "I kept running my pace instead of reacting to the race." "I forgot to put bandaids on my nipples." "I should have asked for her phone number."

For mistakes of omission, there is a clear regret because you failed to act. You need to understand why you didn't make the better decision and figure out how to do better.

These distinctions matter for two reasons. First, not acting and not deciding are two different things. As the rock band Rush put it "If you choose not to decide, you still have made a choice."[79]

Sometimes we fail to act knowingly. Other times we don't even realize a decision has to be made. If this happens it highlights gaps in our systems and training programs.

Second, part of making better mistakes is making mistakes for the right reasons. If we are pushing ourselves to do more, taking on more risk, and testing our limits, we are likely to make many mistakes of commission.

Four Types of Mistakes

---

[79] The song is Freewill. The singer is Neil Peart. But you knew that.

I group mistakes into four buckets, based on what type of mistake they are, and how easy or difficult they are to correct. Mistakes of Omission tend to be caused by Laziness, Distraction, Fear, or Stress. Mistakes of Commission tend to be caused by either Ignorance or Striving.

Ability to Correct

		Easier	Harder
Omission		Laziness & Distraction	Fear & Stress
Type			
Commission		Ignorance	Striving

Fig 46 · Mistakes typically fall into four main types based on why we make them and how correctable they are

Laziness & Distraction

Within this category are all mistakes related to lack of attention and preparation. Maybe you don't care, maybe you have other things on your mind, or maybe your "lazy default" needs some improving. The result: you fail to do what you need to do.

If this is you, start with this question: *what do you hope to get out of your running?*

Laziness is a habit. It's a behavior just like any other, and like other behaviors it becomes something we stop actively considering. Again, it takes three weeks to create a habit and three days to break it. You *can* overcome laziness. It starts with creating newer, more effective systems.

> "You *can* overcome laziness. It starts with creating newer, more effective systems."

We covered distraction when we talked about the "What-We-Think-About-Most-Of-The-Time" Scale. Most distractions don't need your attention at that moment. But let's imagine something really is important. If you can resolve it immediately, do it. Just get it over with.

If you can't resolve it, write it down and schedule a time to come back to it. This has two benefits. First, you get back your focus for your purposeful practice. Second, *not* focusing on it will often help you resolve it. Mentally letting go frees up your subconscious to deal with it better.

Carelessness and disorganization are the end result of these mistakes. Forgotten uniforms, alarms not set, arriving late because you didn't anticipate traffic. It's obvious to see when someone is making Lazy mistakes. The solution starts with taking responsibility and adopting better systems.

Fear / Stress

We often find ourselves in situations where we are uncomfortable, at risk, or in some way threatened. This triggers a feeling of stress or fear (often both). The more fear or stress we feel, the more we avoid making decisions.

Fortunately, running isn't filled with many life-threatening situations. But when our teammates are counting on us? When our family and friends are in the stands? When we've publicly stated what our goals are? In those instances we can feel a lot of pressure to have a good performance.

Even the best runners eventually find themselves in a situation they are not used to. An Olympic 1500 meter final is super stressful! And when your lifelong dream to win a gold medal can hinge on your split-second reactions to a dynamic and constantly changing situation in front of a billion people...it's easy to freeze up.

Fear and stress are difficult to overcome. At a basic level, it requires increasing your self-efficacy. Athletes with high self-efficacy contain their fear and stress by focusing on how hard they've prepared, how ready they are, and how others like them have succeeded in the past.

But that isn't enough. It also takes a lot of preparation. You need a plan for every scenario you can imagine. You need to identify the fear and stress coming from external sources and work to limit their influence. And most of all you need to get reps in these situations (real or simulated).

It's not easy, but fear and stress can be overcome. Don't be afraid to talk about it and work on it.

Ignorance

The simplest and most common reason we make mistakes is because we don't know better. We've never thought about something, we assumed one thing is like another but it's not, somebody told us the wrong information, or what we thought used to be true but the situation changed.

Ignorance is part of life. You'll never know everything. But with some targeted preparation and a willingness to put in the effort, you can eliminate the most obvious ignorant mistakes. Or you can follow the more common path, which is to make the mistake and then realize you were ignorant!

I learned a painful lesson in my first collegiate cross country race. After warming up, all the runners changed into their racing flats. I noticed nobody was wearing socks. Even though I'd always run with socks, I figured they knew something I didn't. I distinctly remember wondering how much faster going sock-less would make me.

About a mile into the dusty, hilly race my feet were uncomfortable. By half-way my feet were burning, especially running downhill. The last two miles were awful. Every stride felt like I was ripping off my skin.

It turns out I was. After the race I took off bloody shoes. I had ripped off two-inch long blisters from the tips of my big toes to the balls of my feet. I had never conditioned my feet to running without socks, and it was a big mistake to try it for the first time in a race.

In my case, ignorance hurt. A lot.

Correcting for ignorance starts with engagement. Look for opportunities to ask questions and understand more. We will never eliminate mistakes of ignorance, but we can limit them by preparing better.

Striving

Striving mistakes happen when you try to do something for the first time. When you push your limits, aspire to more and... don't get everything right. Striving mistakes are related to mistakes of ignorance, but they are more challenging.

Striving mistakes are often the result of "too much too soon." I suffered from stress fractures twice my freshman year because I upped my mileage and intensity too quickly. In both cases, I was striving to train with people above my level and ignored the signs that I was overdoing it. When we are ambitious, it can be hard to find that line between enough and too much.

With striving mistakes, identifying the root cause is the challenge. On the surface it can seem obvious, like when you overdo it in a workout.

But don't stop there. Keep asking more questions: why were you running so much? Was it a problem of volume or pace? Did you sense you were pushing your limits but ignore the signs? Were there other things going on in your life that you should have accounted for (i.e. lack of sleep)?

If the problem is the training program, identify it and make the necessary changes. If it is a question of effort, ensure you are aligning to your Next Step goals.

I told the story in Chapter 4 about changing my training program from tempo runs to fartleks and how much I thought it affected me. It's easy to see now that I was making some critical mistakes due to ignorance and laziness: I didn't understand the big picture; I didn't communicate effectively; I didn't take responsibility; and I was too conservative, convinced the change was an unnecessary risk.

Risk and Performance Rewards

Striving mistakes are a risk every athlete must accept. Doing something you've never done involves risk. But that's ok. Risk is tied to reward.

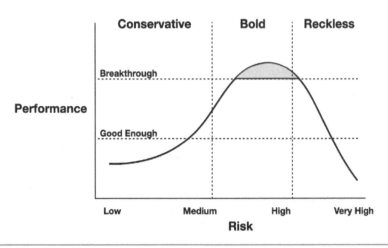

Fig 47 - Achieving a breakthrough performance requires taking on risk; Bold runners plan to take on risk.

The above chart visualizes the relationship between Risk and Performance. Risk is divided into three sections: Conservative, Bold, and Reckless. Performance has two thresholds: Good Enough and Breakthrough.

The solid line shows the potential reward for the amount of risk you take on.

The Risk Line and Performance

Good Enough signifies any performance that won't get you criticized after the fact. You cruise because you have no competition. You are training through. You went for it and struggled at the end but hung on well enough. Whether or not you are happy is more a function of your expectations than the outcome.

Breakthrough means everything went as well as you could have hoped. You did something special. You approached your potential for that day. We often think of this as norm-referenced success (faster times, a better place) but it doesn't have to be. My breakthrough race showed me how much discomfort I could put myself through.

"Striving" is about taking on risk and pursuing a break-through. In the short term, that means a personal best or a great finish. In the medium term this means making a leap.

Our ability to make a leap is tied to our ability to manage risk.

How Much Risk is Too Much?

Conservative: Being conservative does not mean "going out slow." It means trying to eliminate the downside over pursuing the upside.

In the long term, conservative runners don't increase their mileage, avoid races against superior competition, and set only "realistic" goals. In the short-term, they run at a "manageable" pace, don't chase the leaders, and aim to ensure a Good Enough race.

They tend toward making mistakes of omission, because they are avoiding the risk that comes with bold action.

The biggest problem: conservative runners never learn any-thing about themselves. They execute comfortable race plans to achieve Good Enough results. But why?

If you are too conservative, it's for one of these reasons:
- You have a fear of failure
- You have a fear of pain
- Your goal doesn't feel realistic in the moment

If you have a fear of failure, change the goal. In fact, stop fo-cusing on the final place or time altogether. Judge the perfor-mance on how well you execute the plan. Free yourself from the tyranny of norm-referenced expectation!

If you have a fear of pain, well, you may have chosen the wrong sport... More seriously, be confident that increasing your risk isn't the same as being reckless. You won't crash and burn.

Your natural conservative tendencies will ensure that doesn't happen.

Lastly we all set (or agree to) goals we don't truly believe we can accomplish. We have to be mentally ready to do what we set out for. How many elite athletes ask for a fast rabbit but then don't follow them from the gun? What seems bold before the race can seem reckless on the starting line. If you find yourself making last-minute decisions to be more conservative, you need to set better goals.

How to tell if you're too Conservative:
- You expect the worst in your races
- You won't take a chance even when a race isn't going well
- All of your races can be described using the words "decent," "ok," "solid," and "not that bad"
- Your training log shows the same training year after year after year
- You know you can accomplish all of your goals

Reckless: Switching to the other side of our risk spectrum, we find the Reckless runners. In the long-term, Reckless runners over-train, set unrealistic goals (and often *only* unrealistic goals), and train by emotion rather than reason. In the short-term, they enter races with no strategy, run at the front no matter who is in the race, and approach the day's race with an "all or nothing" mentality.

Whereas Conservative runners overthink their races, Reckless runners rarely think at all. As soon as the gun goes off, they get swept up in the moment. They tend toward mistakes of commission, doing or trying too much.

When they rein that emotion in, they can produce excellent results. When they can't, they get passed by everyone in the field. Perhaps most frustrating is their typical response when you call them on it: "You don't understand, I felt so good out there. It wasn't until the end that I felt terrible." Duh.

When it comes to racing, however, Reckless runners have an advantage over Conservative runners. Reckless runners put themselves in position for a breakthrough performance every time. (They typically believe every time will be that time.) Most of their performances will be far better or far worse than those of Conservative runners, with a few being Breakthroughs and many being complete disasters.

How to tell if you're too Reckless:
- You lead every race, but blow up in many of them
- You never know if today's the day for a PR or DNF (but you accept these as likely outcomes)
- You rarely win but always get your picture in the newspaper because of your blazing fast starts
- Your teammates wager on which lap you will fall apart
- You don't stick to your training schedule because you often "feel good"

Bold: It can be hard to see the difference between Bold and Reckless, especially for those of us stuck in a Conservative frame of mind. But there is a difference.

Reckless is emotional. Bold is rational. You can plan to be Bold. You can acknowledge that a Bold race is what it will take to achieve your goal and you can prepare accordingly. You can imagine scenarios and create contingency plans for them.

Will everything go as planned? No. But if it goes badly, you will still run Good Enough. That will be baked into the plan.

If you've prepared and you believe you can do it, then you will put yourself in position to have a breakthrough. And that is all you can do. If it doesn't happen, you chalk one up to experience and try to learn from it for the next race.

How do you know you're a Bold runner:
- You often run personal or seasonal bests, and rarely have terrible races
- You are willing and prepared to make a decisive move mid-race
- You know exactly where you want to be in a race and have a plan for getting there

- You are considered an aggressive runner who is always in control
- You seek to increase your mileage and intensity over time
- You have borderline unrealistic goals, but you have a clear plan to achieve them
- You refuse to settle for "Good Enough"

Strategies: I was too conservative when I was racing competitively. I sacrificed the potential for a great race in order to avoid a terrible race.

Many of my teammates were too reckless. They went for the great race and often finished terribly. Perhaps if we'd considered the relationship between risk and reward better we would have been able to change some of our tendencies.

Here are a few ideas that may help you overcome your tendency to be either too conservative or too reckless, to find that Bold middle ground.

- After you set your race goal, commit to making it 4/5 of the race at your goal pace or in your goal position. Even on a bad day, you should be able to make it 4/5 of the way.
- Practice different behavior when it doesn't matter. Small invitationals are a great place for conservative athletes to be a little reckless, and reckless athletes to be a little conservative. Since nothing crucial hinges on the results, use the opportunity to try something new.
- Then again, when everything is on the line, there is a lot of opportunity for someone willing to take a risk. The more important the result, the more conservative people get. Underdogs create upsets by realizing they have nothing to lose and taking a bold risk.[80]
- Anticipate and accept the possibility of failure. Risk and failure also go hand in hand. Evaluate your performance on your effort and execution, not just the final time or place.

---

[80] This was how Meb won the Boston Marathon. He saw that the pace was too conservative and he made a break. Other runners assumed he was being reckless and let him go. It turns out it was a bold, calculated move, and in the end nobody was able to catch him.

- Don't equate how you feel in practice today with how you will feel in a future race. (Rarely a problem for Reckless runners!)
- Consult with your coach and develop a racing strategy you believe in. Utilize your strengths (i.e. thoughtfulness for Conservative runners, aggressiveness for Reckless runners) but make sure they don't dictate your strategy.
- Talk to teammates who have figured it out. Ask them how they approach their races.

One more thing to keep in mind: being conservative to avoid mistakes is often the riskiest thing you can do.

> *"Being conservative to avoid mistakes is often the riskiest thing you can do."*

Mistakes Sustain Momentum

You make a leap when you maintain your momentum and positive feedback loops. So how do we reconcile mistakes as positive when they slow our progress?

We aren't seeking perfection, we're seeking improvement. And we won't always know if there's a way to improve unless we try new things. That's why Striving mistakes are valuable (even if they result in temporary setbacks) and other types of mistakes (Fear, Stress, Laziness, Ignorance) are less valuable.

Mistakes in themselves are not shameful. How we handle them can be. Be bold, strive to continually improve, and when you make a mistake, course correct and learn from it.

Key Takeaways

1. A mistake of commission occurs because of your direct action. A mistake of omission occurs because you failed to take action. Both result from choices.

2. There are many types of mistakes, but the most valuable are Striving mistakes. These are mistakes you make because you are trying to do something new, pushing beyond your previous experiences.

3. Risk is an essential element of optimal training. It is best to approach your training with a Bold strategy that includes some risk along with a clear plan to achieve your goal.

11. Analysis: Where Are You Now?

You are practicing purposefully. You've created systems to improve your discipline. You're striving to be better and taking on bold risks. What next?

You need to interpret your results and make new decisions.

Did that workout go as planned? Did the past week or month see the kind of progress you were hoping for? Do you feel any differently now that you've incorporated these changes?

There are times when training goes perfectly. It's magical.

There are also times when training becomes a slog, where you are working hard but don't seem to be making any progress. It's very much un-magical.

Yet both of these are normal and lead us to the next Optimal Training Principle.

OTP #10: Racing times and personal records indicate progress at one point in time.

Every leap looks the same. Progress is slow, slow, slow, slow, and then boom, it jumps up a level. But this creates a problem. How do you know if you're on track? How do you know your slow progress isn't just slow progress?

You need to have a grasp on both where you are and how fast you are moving. That means having an idea of what is working and what needs improvement.

When you are looking at the big picture, it's best to focus on quality of execution. Remember, your leap will be based on the quality of your feedback loop, and that has to repeat over and over. Anything affecting that will hold you back.

When analyzing specific races or practices, it's again important to focus on quality. In this case, it means focusing on execution over results. You can win a poorly run race and you can lose an excellently run race. Results often hide the important takeaways.

The following may be obvious, but they are useful tools for analyzing your training.

Keep a Daily Activity Log

When I was at Apple, my team went through a stretch where we were feeling overwhelmed and unproductive. It seemed like we were working non-stop but the highest value items on our to-do lists were never getting done. We decided to keep detailed track of our time to see if we could figure out why.

It confirmed something shocking: we were being interrupted by other people 30 or so times per day! Many of these interruptions were important and it was our team's job to address them. But these requests didn't come at specific times. They came when they came. The result: we were *constantly distracted*.

Having this info was a huge help. It not only confirmed we needed to make some changes, but it helped us to identify exactly where we could get the most benefit. We put new systems in place to reduce the minute-to-minute distraction.

How does this work from a training perspective?

	Group (Optional)	Activity	Comment
7:00	Sleep / Rest	Sleep	Woke up 7:10
7:15	Training	Core / Stretching	Stretching
7:30	Training	Morning Run	
7:45	Training	Morning Run	30 mins regular loop, solo, legs tight
8:00	Training	Core / Stretching	Sit-ups, Stretching
8:15	Other	Shower	
8:30	Diet	Breakfast	Bagel w/cream cheese; coffee
8:45	Entertainment	Instagram	Need to call mom
9:00	School	Bike to school	
9:15	School	Bike to school	So many bad drivers!
9:30	School	Class	Micromobility 101: Scooters and Bikes
9:45	School	Class	
10:00	School	Class	Very tired, almost fell asleep
10:15	School	Class	Hungry!
10:30	Diet	Snack	Protein bar

Fig 48 - A simple daily activity log using 15 minute increments and three columns

Keep a record of everything you are doing throughout the day. Track your time in 15-minute increments (this gives the most insight for the amount of effort...80/20!). Round up or down as necessary. Create some general buckets: rest, training, diet, school, work, chores, relaxing, etc. No more than ten.

The simplest approach is to use three columns. In the first, note the general category. In the second, put whatever you were actually doing. In the third, include a comment or note to add context. If you do two things at once—like washing dishes and listening to podcasts—assign the time to the more active activity and put a comment about the passive activity.

This probably feels like a lot, but you *don't* have to do this forever. To get the 80/20 benefits from this activity, do it for two weeks. Just make sure they are typical weeks—no vacations or illnesses—so that you can make good assumptions based on what you record. Everybody is surprised by something when they do this.

As for comments, take notice of how you feel during the day. Are you especially hungry, thirsty, tired, lazy, sleepy, stressed? Note it down as a comment. It might signal something important about your routines.

Group	Mon	Tue	Wed	Thu
Sleep / Rest	7.5	7	7.5	7
Training	5	4.5	5	4.5
School	5	4.25	4.5	4
Diet	2	2.5	2	2.75
Entertainment	3	4.5	4	5
Other	1.5	1.25	1	0.75
Total	**24**	**24**	**24**	**24**

Fig 49 - An activity log summary to see how our days are being spent

Keep track of what foods you are eating. Look for patterns around what, when, and how much you consume.

Are you doing everything at the same times each day? Or are you skipping an activity for lack of time? Positive feedback loops depend on consistency.

Now group things up and see how you are spending your time. How much time do you spend on unproductive or neutral activities? Where are you constantly rushing? Where are you procrastinating? Is there something you are doing that is actually unhealthy or that you simply don't like? These are perfect candidates for new systems.

Don't try to document your life perfectly. Keep it an 80/20 activity. Track just enough to get an idea of what's really going on.

Most people report two benefits on top of the insights into their time. First, they act more focused because they know they have to track the results. They improve so that the results look better. This is standard observation effect.

Second, if you do this for two weeks you will feel much more engaged and responsible. This is important. Positive attitudes reinforce their own feedback loops.

Monthly Momentum Model

For taking stock of my situation in its entirety, I always fall back on the Momentum Model. The reason is simple. Where I'm at isn't that important. Where I'm heading and how fast I'm moving is.

How we feel about our situation is less about where we are and more about what direction we are moving. If you think tomorrow is looking better than today, you'll feel good. If your situation isn't what you want and you see no means to change it, you'll be dissatisfied.

> *"How we feel about our situation is less about where we are and more about what direction we are moving."*

Here's a simple system to build the Momentum Model into your monthly routine. Each month, fill out the model and give the arrows whatever value makes sense to represent their relative strength. Be as honest and objective as you can about it. This is for you. There's no need to share it.

Now, you already know where you are and how you were performing a month ago, three months ago, etc. Look at your monthly Momentum Models and see how they are changing. Do the changes align with your current performance? Are you driving those changes or is something else in your environment? Are you accurately analyzing the factors contributing to your momentum?

Now look at the Momentum Model you just filled out. Pick a couple arrows to improve. Either create a better system or figure out how to better apply the principles of Purposeful Practice to it. Always start with the bigger arrows. You'll get more bang for your buck.

A Monthly Momentum Model is a system for creating better systems. Use your progress *at this point in time* to drive you to your future goals.

Improving Our Analysis Generally

The Daily Activity Log and Monthly Momentum Model are two proven approaches you can use to analyze your situation. To return to our "the brain is a prediction factory" mental model, those systems improve the machinery in our factory. They increase the likelihood that our predictions will be accurate.

We can also improve the feedback we are receiving. Feedback is one of the raw materials in our prediction factory. High quality feedback contributes to high quality output. And vice versa.

Attribution Errors About Yourself and Others

Let's return to attribution theory, because attribution errors create some of the biggest errors in our analysis.

Attribution theory explains the differences between the way high achievers and low achievers attribute success and failure. As you recall, high achievers tend to view results through the lens of effort, whereas low achievers do not.

There is a related concept called Fundamental Attribution Error that leads us to attribute others' actions poorly. We tend to be hyper-aware of external factors that affect our own behavior. But we ignore those same factors when we attribute behavior to others. We assume that "what they do represents who they are."

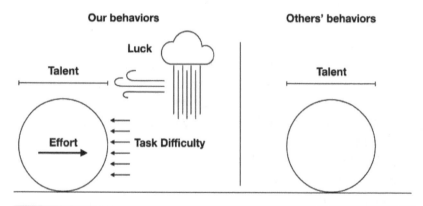

Fig 50 - Fundamental Attribution Error and Talent Trap associate all performance with talent, and neglect other key factors

Imagine you are preparing for a race and doing warm-up drills. You say, "Good luck," to a competitor but they don't acknowledge you. Why not?

We frequently attribute other people's responses to something internal to them. Clearly they're a "jerk." But if the situation were reversed, we would deny that we are a jerk and instead say it was due to the situation, that we were "focused."

This example is trivial unless the brushed off individual loses and gets inspired to train harder with the express purpose of beating "the jerk" in the future.[81]

This is even more relevant when we consider other people's race performances. We naturally attribute their performances to who they are, a.k.a. their talent. I call this the "talent trap" and it affects so many athletes. Someone beats us and we assume they have more talent than we do.

When someone beats you, it means they were better than you *on that day*. It does not mean they have more talent or work harder than you or that the race was easier for them or that they got lucky. It is one result at one point in time. There is nothing fixed about it that carries forward to the future, except that you may have some ground to make up to reach their current ability level.

If they are training hard, you need to train even harder. If they are preparing well, you need to prepare even better. Their performance is also just an indication of their progress at one point in time, so there's nothing stopping them from increasing the gap as well.

Making Criticism Constructive

Not all feedback is praise. You need critical feedback to point out where you can get better. You need to be able to do this yourself, but this is *the key area* where having a coach helps. A

---

[81] Yes the brushed off individual was me, and yes I finally beat the guy two years later. I no longer believe he was a jerk, but I cannot deny it inspired me greatly when I raced against him.

good coach will tailor effective and fair criticism to the personality of each runner.

Criticism comes in all forms. Sometimes it is thoughtful and nuanced: "If you can learn to recognize when the gap is going to close you can keep from getting boxed in. Don't be afraid to make a move, you have more room than you think."

Other times it's blunt: "What the $^%& was that?"

When you receive criticism, try not to judge the specific words. Rule #1 of communication: most people aren't good at it. You can't assume the way people express themselves is carefully thought out and perfectly tailored for the message they are trying to express. Often it's just the first thing that came to their mind.

"Rule #1 of communication: most people aren't good at it."

Always separate the message from how you feel. Ask whether their main message is fair or unfair. If you feel it's unfair, think about why. Is the person making a fundamental attribution error? Is there context that they are missing? Did something about your action look worse than it really was?

Seeing the world from another person's perspective is a super power. People often see what they are looking for and ignore what they aren't interested in.[82] By considering who is giving you feedback, you can also understand why they are giving you this specific feedback.

Sometimes feedback isn't helpful. Keep in mind that most people who give you criticism *are* trying to help you. They may not be doing a good job of it, but in that case you can convert it to serve your purposes.

Take it upon yourself to make feedback constructive. First, ignore criticism that is centered on you as a person. Nobody should be telling you that you have no potential or that you are a

---

[82] In psychology this is called confirmation bias.

bad person. Keep that nonsense out of your head (and out of your life if possible).

For all other criticism, convert it into effort-based terms. It's not that helpful to describe a performance as "bad," "weak," "scared," "clueless," "embarrassing," or "Gawdawful." (Those may be true, but they give you nothing to work with.)

I propose the following conversions:

- Bad –> "poorly executed"
- Scared –> "too conservative"
- Weak –> "lacking in effort"
- Clueless –> "unprepared"
- Embarrassing –> "obviously lacking in preparation and effort"
- Gawdawful –> "terribly executed"

Effort is the one factor we can control. It doesn't make sense to analyze our results against any other factor.

> *"Effort is the one factor we can control. It doesn't make sense to analyze our results against any other factor."*

If there was some unexpected bad luck or difficulty you couldn't prepare for (getting tripped in the race, for example) then you can acknowledge it. But the focus should be on how you can prepare for and work your way through the situation in the future.

"Respect your position while preparing for your promotion."

I love this quote by Jalen Rose, a former NBA basketball player and current ESPN analyst. He often uses it when someone is upset they aren't getting what they feel they deserve. It is a great mantra for your career and for running.

In optimal training terms: *respect your current ability while preparing for your future success.*

Respect your position: You are where you are. How far that is from your goals is not an indication of whether you can achieve them, but rather how hard you have to work to get there.

Maybe you are the best on your team and on the cusp of being the best in the country. Maybe you are a middle-of-the-pack runner searching for consistent success. Or maybe you are struggling to perform at the same level you ran last year, recovering from an injury, or dealing with some other issues that are hindering your performance.

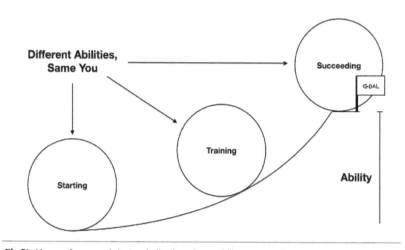

Fig 51 - Your performance is just an indication of your ability at a specific point in time

Fine. You are where you are. Acknowledge it and train accordingly.

With that said, you are not your latest performance. Your performance is a reflection of your ability *at this point in time.* That's it.

Respecting your current ability does not mean tying your identity to it. If you believe you have the ability to run sub-four for the mile, but you currently run 4:20, that doesn't mean sub-four is impossible. It means you can't do it "right now." Something needs to change to get you to your goal.

You may need to make life changes. You may need to change your training program. You may need to do a little less now, improve your feedback loop, and then do more later. Or maybe you just need to stay the course, and the improvement will come with time.

Filling out your momentum model will help you identify if obvious changes are necessary.

Remember: If you build the right feedback loops and execute consistently, where you are in three months can look nothing like where you are today.

Prepare for your promotion: How are you going to get from here to there, from now to tomorrow, from who you are today to who you want to be? And how are you going to stay there?

Those are the fundamental questions you need to be answering. You can't prepare for your future success without having some idea how far away from achieving it you are.

Above all, you can't wait to become excellent before you start living the lifestyle necessary to sustain excellence. As Jon Rankin puts it, "You need *to be* that person before you become that person."

*"You need **to be** that person before you become that person."*

Great runners structure their lives around their training. They do this long before they actually achieve any success. If you want to be great, you need to think, train, and live like you already are.

I can't prescribe for you the training program that will get you to your goal. For that you need to talk with your coach. But I can tell you how you will need to approach it. You will need to:

- Focus on understanding your training, via discussing, reading and sharing ideas
- Take personal responsibility for all aspects of your training

- Improve your self-efficacy by studying how you and your peers overcame obstacles in the past
- Believe that your ability tomorrow will be changed by your behavior today
- Painstakingly prepare before, during and after your workouts
- Create new systems that improve your feedback loops, especially around sleeping, eating, and managing your other responsibilities
- Make lots of bold, striving mistakes (but avoid injury!)
- Commit to and communicate your goals with other people
- Dedicate yourself to Purposeful Practice, Next Step goals, and developing your ability to concentrate, receive feedback, and push your limits

The result of your analysis should be activities like these. It should identify the biggest areas for improvement, with an emphasis on 80/20 changes. Find the lowest hanging fruit and pick it.

No matter how long you've been training, you're still just at a point on the path toward your next goal. Whether you are at the beginning or the end, there is always room to improve. Do the work to understand how you got here and what you need to do next.

Identifying those opportunities and executing on them is what it's all about.

Key Takeaways

1. It is important to not get fixated on your performances in the moment. They are only indications of where you are at a single point in time.

2. Be careful how you attribute the success of others. It is easy to fall into a fallacy of thinking others are succeeding because of their talent alone.

3. Translate criticism into effort-based terms. It will be easier to apply it constructively to your training.

4. The point of all your analysis is to prepare you to achieve your future goals. Develop excellent behaviors now to achieve excellent results in the future. Act as if.

12. Perseverance: Sticking With It

Kara Goucher is one of the most accomplished distance runners in US history.[83] But her path to the top was far from a straight line. She had multiple periods where her performances were far below her expectations.

Kara graduated from the University of Colorado in 2000 as a 3-time NCAA Champion, winning the 3k/5k double on the track and the women's individual cross country title the next fall (in quite possibly the worst weather in NCAA meet history).[84]

She then spent the next five years training through numerous injuries and setbacks until finally running another personal best in 2006!

---

[83] Kara is a two-time Olympian, World Championships 10k silver medalist, 3-time NCAA Champion, and one of the fastest US marathoners all-time. Her bio: http://www.karagoucher.com/statistics/

[84] I also competed at that meet. It was 17 degrees Fahrenheit, had gusty 30 mph winds, hailed briefly, and I finished the race with icicles on my eyelashes. Kara was prepared and won her race. I was not and finished 120th.

This was not an easy time. As Kara described it,[85] "It was hard. I'm not gonna lie. I mean, I passed up a post-graduate scholarship to run professionally and I would be on the elliptical for two hours a day being like, 'I could be somebody, you know, I could do something,' you know what I mean?

"But the thing was every time I thought about quitting I knew I would regret it. I just knew it. I just, I knew that I had more and I would just get this pit in my stomach and I would be like, 'I have to keep trying.'"

Kara made a lot of changes in pursuit of her running dreams. She and her husband moved from Boulder, Colorado to Portland, Oregon. She changed coaches and adopted entirely new training programs. She underwent surgeries, rehabbed, and recovered.

And finally, it clicked and she made a huge leap.

"The biggest life lesson I've gotten out of running is patience. Things take time. I can't tell you how many times I was on the sidelines watching people *I knew I was just as good as* getting attention or winning races. And I was just like, my time will come.

"You can't quit because you don't get it right away. That's running. *That is running.* Running is, the more years you stay healthy, the better it gets. So you have to commit for the long haul."

> "You can't quit because you don't get it right away. That's running. **That is running.**"

Kara calls it patience. I call it perseverance. Regardless, Kara stuck with it. She overcame her obstacles. She got herself healthy, built a world-class feedback loop and put in the work.

She could have quit at any time and nobody would have questioned her. But she knew the work she was putting in was building to something, and she had the patience to see it through.

---

[85] In an interview on the Go Be More Podcast on 8/14/2020.

OTP #11: Optimal performances and realizing your potential are results of painstaking preparation and hard work.

Your goal should be to realize your potential. To run as fast as your physical and mental talents will permit. Every other goal is a milestone on that journey.

In order to realize your potential, you first need to improve on a shorter time frame. Let's imagine you have the potential to be Olympic Champion. In order to achieve that goal, you first need to reach the level of a national champion. But before that a collegiate champion. But before that a conference champion. But before that the fastest on your team. And so on.

We can keep going backwards but it eventually stops at one place: you need to run your best. Today. Tomorrow. Everyday.

The mindsets we adopt and the environment we create will ultimately determine whether or not we run our best. So we need to prepare and work hard with a focus on those areas.

I think of it like this: Build momentum today. Sustain momentum tomorrow.

Building Momentum Today = Think Big

Painstaking preparation is about engagement and decision-making. It requires understanding where you are, what you need to do, and how you're going to do it.

You need to prioritize. You need to get the big things right, because it's the big things that most determine our momentum and progress.

You should have a good handle on the positive and negative forces affecting your training. The quickest way to improve will always be to take an 80/20 approach and target the strongest forces in your life, whether those are positive or negative.

A small change to a big force often has a larger effect than a big change to a small force. To quickly boost momentum today, focus on the biggest arrows in your Momentum Model.

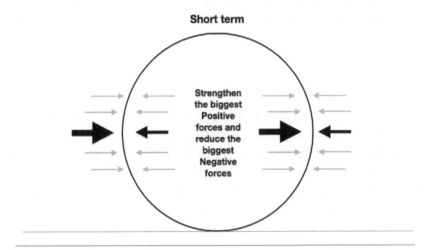

Short term

Strengthen the biggest Positive forces and reduce the biggest Negative forces

Fig 52 - Short term: identify and improve all of the biggest forces affecting your performance

Large Internal Forces

Our effort and our preparation are internal variables that we can control. We must start here.

In the spotlight on Next Level 80/20 we identified consistent effort and purposeful practice as the activities that have the greatest impact on our results. They need to be your strongest internal forces.

Most athletes' approach to practice is positive but has a lot of room for improvement. Remember the cornerstones of purposeful practice: set better Next Step goals, get better feedback, improve your ability to concentrate, and develop specific skills in every workout. Take the time, actively consider everything you are doing, and put in the hard work to train more purposefully.

Active engagement is key. Get more involved, learn more, and share your goals with friends and colleagues. These are simple activities you can do today. They will boost your accountability and the quality of your effort.

Discuss your short- to medium-term training schedule with your coach. The best way to stay on a path is to use a map. Ask your coach to let you see the map. Understand your benchmarks, align your expectations, and get focused on the Next Step goals for each day. Strive to turn this into a system that empowers you and strengthens your relationship.

Your health is another area that needs to be strongly positive. If you are healthy, then put in place systems to stay that way. If you have simple areas for improvement, start doing them now because your health affects everything else you are trying to do.

Many of us have chronic health issues we need to manage. Take responsibility to figure out the treatment you need and stick to the regimen your doctor recommends. For some issues, medicine may be the only answer. But for many health related issues our lifestyles, diets and daily behaviors have a huge impact. Find what works for you and prioritize a lifestyle that maximizes your health.

This goes for your mental health, too. You will never achieve your potential if your mind is holding you back. If depression, anxiety, lack of confidence, stress, or distraction are major problems, it's time to take action now.

There is no shame in seeking help for your mental health. All elite athletes work with professional sports psychologists and counselors. If you need help and aren't getting it, you are simply putting yourself at a disadvantage.

*"You **can** create new habits of thought."*

I've provided you the key tools you need to evaluate your training and many of your day-to-day activities. They will help you build the habits of thought and behavior you need. Yes, *you can create new habits of thought*. Here's a simple one: make a rule to never use the word "talented" to describe somebody's performance. Whenever you want to say the word, substitute it with "hard-working."[86]

The key to battling large negative internal forces is to recognize that *they are not fixed*. If you can identify them, you can improve them. Even a small change can be enough to create a huge improvement if maintained for enough time.

Large External Forces

Once we've got our biggest internal forces in order, it's time to focus on the environment around us.

The single biggest improvement you can make to your training is to remove large negative external forces. Pushing harder isn't the only way to increase momentum. Removing barriers and friction helps, too.

External forces can pose a difficult challenge. They are tied up with our social lives. Our partners, managers, children, parents, and friends. Our classes, work deliverables, and parental responsibilities. Our communities, both physical and digital. Cutting them completely out of our lives isn't always possible.

There is one situation, however, where it is necessary. Life-threatening problems must be addressed immediately. If you are battling addiction, abuse, or an external threat like the coronavirus you must deal with it now.

For everything else, focus on reducing the negative effect. The biggest decision I made prior to making a leap was to stop going out drinking with friends. I probably cut out 95% of my nights out. This one decision improved my diet, my sleep, and how I felt each morning. It also reinforced my perception of myself as a dedicated athlete striving to be my best. I took a small negative arrow (I didn't drink that much) and turned it into a medium-sized positive arrow.

Did I miss some crazy nights? Yes. Do I regret that now. Not one bit.

---

[86] In my experience, 50% of people scoff at this idea and refuse to even consider it. They see it as being intellectually dishonest. It's not. You aren't denying the existence of talent. You're just choosing to view success through the lens of effort.

If your friends are pushing you to stay out late, you *can* opt to stay in. I give you permission. Tell them it's because you are making a bet on yourself and you intend to win it. They won't like it, but if you have a reason and stick to it they will accept it.

If you are overwhelmed with schoolwork, you can create new systems to improve how you study. If you are struggling to connect with your coach, you can initiate a conversation. Whatever the problem is, no matter how big it feels, *there is always a way to improve it*. Dig in and find it.

> *"Whatever the problem is, no matter how big it feels, **there is always a way to improve it.**"*

On the flip side, you also need to have some strong positive support if you're going to achieve your goals.

Hopefully you have many strong positive forces in your life. The more the better. I always recommend you take some time to show your gratitude to your biggest supporters. Say thank you!

In general, I don't recommend putting a lot of effort into improving relationships that are already strongly positive. You're better served reducing negative forces or improving your purposeful practice.

However, there are two relationships every athlete should aim to strengthen. The first is your relationship with your coach. Athletes who are at odds with their coaches under-perform. They just do. It is your job to get the most out of your coach.

The second is to find a mentor. A good mentor is like a guide. They will be more experienced than you and willing to use that experience to help you navigate your journey. They must be willing to allocate a small amount of time to your progress and success.

The mentor's role is to provide feedback, assess your progress, and discuss whatever is on your mind. A coach can be a mentor, of course. But one benefit of having a different mentor is their ability to help you navigate your relationship with your coach!

When dealing with your mentor it's your responsibility to have specific, thoughtful questions for them to answer.

- **Bad:** "How do I get faster?"
- **Better:** "I'm going to the XX race in a couple weeks. Do you have any advice for what I should expect?"
- **Best:** "I'm going to the XX race in a couple weeks. I have done YY and plan to do ZZ leading up to the race. I'm worried about ABC. Can you provide me any guidance or advice based on what I've done and my latest plans?

Mentoring is an idea that has gained traction in the business community but less so within the sports community. This needs to change. A mentor can be invaluable in so many areas: ensuring engagement, gaining perspective, boosting self-efficacy, taking on responsibility, analyzing progress, building effective systems and practicing purposefully. Pretty much everything!

Larger Forces = More Leverage

To review, the key to building momentum today is 1) knowing what areas of your life have an 80/20 effect on your training, and 2) improving those areas strategically.

When I use the word "today" I am referring, of course, to the short-term. You have to spend time and energy to turn them into habits, routines and systems. How long does it take? A couple weeks to a couple months.

It is hard work to create new systems. You have to actively consider what you are doing and how to improve it. You have to change both your mindset and your physical environment, neither of which happen immediately or easily.

Remember that your future effort will build on your current effort. Don't try to do it all now. Focus on making small changes to the biggest, strongest forces.

With each boost in momentum you should feel a little more committed. A little more engaged. A little more motivated. Use those feelings to help make the next small change. And repeat, and repeat, and repeat.

Sustaining Momentum Tomorrow = Think Small & Think All

The biggest forces in our lives–purposeful practice, our mindsets, our health, our coaches and mentors, and anyone significantly holding us back–determine most of our daily progress. That's why it's so important to get those right.

Once you've accomplished that, it's time to get ALL of your arrows in alignment. I call this, "Think Small and Think All."

For every Next Level 80/20 activity, there are dozens of activities that have less impact on our training. The small inconveniences, the distractions, the doubts, the snacks and sweets, the people who come and go. Individually, each one doesn't have much of an effect. But collectively they can make a big difference.

This is the Hidden Training Program. The way we practice drives the majority of our success, but all the little things in our lives are what we actually need to get aligned if we want to reach our potential.

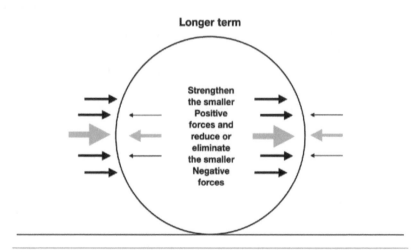

Fig 53 - Long term: focus on improving all of the small arrows (Think Small, Think All)

As we look toward the future, our mindset must be to keep *all our arrows* pointed in the right direction. It's not possible, but framing the challenge in these terms makes it easier to identify what stays and what goes.

Small Internal Forces

If you're like the rest of us, you can improve your physical health, managing your emotions, thinking clearly and productively, maintaining concentration, and believing in your ability to achieve your goals. You can engage a little more, take on a little more responsibility, and manage your time a little better.

As you start tackling the countless small forces that affect your training, remember the basic math of what we're trying to do.

1. One small improvement maintained over time can lead to a small leap.
2. Many small improvements maintained over time can lead to a big leap.

> ## "Many small improvements maintained over time can lead to a big leap."

It's the consistency that matters. Don't worry about perfection, just improvement. The improvement will compound on itself. As each improvement becomes routine you will free up the mental willpower to improve in a new area.

Any improvements you can make to your physical and mental health are worth pursuing. A little more sleep, a little better diet, a little better "lazy default," a little less stress, a little less doubt.

You won't see the changes immediately. But given enough time, they will start to make a difference.

Learning how to think better about your training is another area where there are countless small areas to improve. The more ways you can understand your training, the more tools you will have to overcome the obstacles in your way. You should be continually learning more about the sport. Make it a system.

You can also apply what you are learning elsewhere to the sport. Whether you are an engineer, a poet, a historian or a performer the principles that drive success in your field will relate to your training as well. Find those connections. Explore them. Create them.

The biggest benefit of consistently working on these small forces is the sense of commitment and engagement you create. The more you succeed, the more you define yourself as someone in control of your life and your performances. The more you feel this way, the easier it is to keep doing the necessary work.

Small External Forces

You want to be training in the most positive, supportive environment you can find. The quality of your coach and team environment will have the largest impact on your training. But there will be lots of smaller decisions you also need to get right if you are going to reach your potential.

Are you a social person who wants to be around people? Do you want to be living in a big city or a small town? Will you be working while you train or will you be dedicating all of your energy to your running?

Who you invite into your life matters. Keeping positive, supportive people in your orbit while removing those that hold you back is *a skill*. Start developing it now. You will have to make tough decisions about who gets access to your time, energy, and attention.

*"Keeping positive, supportive people in your orbit while removing those that hold you back **is a skill**. Start developing it now."*

The activities you take on will also affect your training. Getting good grades, volunteering, traveling, networking, researching, applying, interviewing, etc, all take a lot of energy.

You will likely have non-training goals that can start to hold you back. That doesn't mean you should drop them. You will need to have effective systems in place to manage all the time and energy you are putting into them. If you can't make them positive, at least keep them neutral.

These smaller forces are not our top priority in the short-term. But start thinking about them, figure out what environment you will thrive in, and systematically prepare for it.

On Injuries and Other Predictable Obstacles

Building and sustaining momentum is hard work even when there are no major obstacles. Sadly there are always major obstacles, injuries being the most predictable.

You will get injured. Your body is a fine-tuned machine and you don't know its limits. The more you push yourself to be your best, the more you will push beyond your limits. Injuries are natural striving mistakes.

You can still do a lot to avoid them. You can incorporate strength and flexibility exercises into your training. You can do thorough warm-up and cool-down routines. You can get enough sleep and recovery treatment. And you can learn when to take your foot off the gas in order to avoid losing control.

One of the hardest lessons to learn for young runners is the need to strategically back off in order to avoid injury. As I described earlier, I spent much of my freshman year training in the pool due to stress fractures.

I had been there a month or so when Meb chose to cross train in the pool for a couple weeks. He wasn't hurt. He decided to cross train *to avoid the risk of getting hurt*. I didn't even know that was an option.

He also arrived with a detailed workout plan for the pool. He had specific tools, like a flotation belt and "pool shoes" to help him. And he worked out *hard*. He would get his heart rate up above 180, his brow sweating despite being immersed in the cool water.

Those two weeks changed my perspective on injuries and maintaining momentum. Meb's priorities were clear:

- Stay healthy (even if it means backing off)
- Get 100% out of whatever workout you are doing

These align to the rule of thumb I shared earlier: It's better to get 100% out of a good workout than 70% out of a perfect one. This is doubly true if trying to do the perfect workout increases your risk of injury.

Cross-training might reduce your momentum a bit. But getting hurt can stop it completely. Your long-term success will be due to how much your small improvements compound on each other. Consistency trumps all.

The same thing goes for when you do eventually get hurt and suffer a setback. The emphasis needs to be on getting 100% out of your situation. Recovering faster, building healthier systems, and getting what you can out of your workouts. You want to lose as little momentum as possible.

You can prepare for this as well. Develop relationships with the trainers and support network whose help you will need to recover. Know what negative forces in your life are contributing to your injury risk and start reducing them. Build the systems you will need beforehand. One of those is a self-referenced mindset.

When you get injured, your norm-referenced performance will get worse. If that's all you ever focus on, you will be more discouraged and your results will look like failure. But if you have developed a self-referenced mindset you won't need to change anything but the expectation you set for yourself.

Great runners rely on their self-referenced goals to get through the most difficult stretches of their training. The best runners bounce back from injury as fit as ever, because they had already established momentum-sustaining routines and they spent their recovery maximizing them.

More than ever, recovering from injury is when you need to focus on execution over results. Have the confidence that your effort will pay off in regained momentum. Trust that every extra bit of productivity you get out of your actions is making your feedback loop that much stronger.

Patience is a virtue...and transferrable

Kara Goucher has retired from competitive running, but she is still very much active in the sport. She is a leading voice against performance enhancing drugs and the medicalization of the sport. She is also one of the leaders in the fight to improve athlete contracts, especially in the area of women's maternity.

She draws upon everything she learned in her training in tackling these initiatives. "Now as I move forward with trying to change some things in the industry, it takes time," Kara says. "[Running] has helped me just look at my life...[and ask] what is it that I care about now?

"But I remain calm, patient. I'm aware it's going to take time."

Kara knows from experience change doesn't happen immediately, but that when it's time it can happen quickly. So she continues to put in the work, to build the necessary foundation, and to be ready for when the change comes.

When she feels overwhelmed, she backs off and ensures she can give 100%. She knows it's better to occasionally do less in order to sustain high quality work over time. She is focused on getting as many large forces pointing in the right direction as possible.

Patience and perseverance are essential to realizing your potential. But they are also transferrable skills. You can apply them in every aspect of your life.

The same is true for thinking better. Patiently and painstakingly applying the ideas we've discussed will make you a better runner. It will also improve every other aspect of your life. It won't make achieving your goals easy, but it will make it *easier*.

To be the best, you can't just out-work your competition. You need to *out-think* and *out-live* your competition.

*"To be the best, you can't just out-work your competition. You need to **out-think** and **out-live** your competition."*

Believe in yourself and your abilities. Commit to the long haul. Create a positive feedback loop filled with strong internal and external forces. And then be patient and put in the work.

You will make the leap.

Key Takeaways

1. Realizing your potential is the sum of many optimal performances over years and years of training. It doesn't come easily.

2. In the short-term, focus on the biggest factors: purposeful practice, consistent effort, good health, a strong relationship with your coach and mentor, and removing any major negative forces.

3. In the long-term, focus on aligning all the small forces in your life. The sum of these small forces is powerful. The best athletes keep every aspect of their lives as positive as possible.

4. Injuries are an inevitable part of training, and you need to prepare for them. Having a support network in place is critical for getting back on track.

Conclusion: Next Steps

This book is based on one simple premise: the better we think about our training, the better we will train. Think better, train better.

Most athletes put all their energies into their physical training. They fail to appreciate the benefits that can come from *thinking optimally* about their training. I've introduced, explained, and provided examples for the key mindsets and attitudes that lead to optimal training.

Some Rules of Training are Universal

We don't train in a vacuum. Our environment plays an enormous role in our success. The better we understand it, the more able we are to manipulate it to our advantage.

Chapter 1 connected the idea of making a leap to sustaining positive feedback loops. The key takeaway from this chapter is that improvement is not linear. Improvement follows a Build -

Leap - Sustain "LeapCycle," and the Leap phase determines both how much we improve and how quickly. We can't control when we make a leap, but we can create the conditions for one.

The Spotlight on the Momentum Model provided you a means to visualize your positive feedback loops. This model is the best framework for analyzing which forces are helping us and which are holding us back. It is also general enough that nearly every other idea can be applied to it.

Part 1 Recap: The Key Attitudes for Success

In Part 1 we covered the five key attitudes that drive success: engagement, responsibility, a growth mindset, self-efficacy, and mental causation. We also looked at three spotlights on foundational thinking concepts.

Chapter 2 introduced us to the Optimal Training Pyramid and the first of our Optimal Training Principles: *Your athletic performance is a result of your attitude, your effort, and your training methods.* The key insight here is that your effort builds on your attitude, and your training methods refine your effort. Attitude is the foundation of success. You must get this right to be successful.

Chapter 3 discussed engagement. *Active engagement in training makes the process more understandable, more relevant, and more effective. (And more fun.)* Your engagement enhances your passion and motivation, which are essential to sustaining effort. By maintaining a sense of curiosity and perspective, you will discover the Hidden Training Program and understand what you *really* need to do to be successful.

Responsibility was the theme of Chapter 4. *You are responsible for your own training.* Athletes often delegate all responsibility for planning and analysis to their coach, and focus solely on execution. That won't work if you aim to be great. You are responsible for getting the best out of your coach.

The short Spotlight on Attribution Theory introduced the way high and low achievers think about their performance. Across all fields, high achievers attribute their successes and failures to their effort. Low achievers focus on external causes for their success and lack of talent for their failures. How you talk about your performances reinforces how you think about them. Talk better, think better. How do we do this? Start with Green's Razor: "Never attribute to talent or luck that which is adequately explained by effort."

Chapter 5 introduced the concept of a growth mindset. *Ability is a variable, not a constant. The harder you work, the more able you become.* If you are willing to put in the work, you can get better at anything. We also broke down the differences between norm-referenced and self-referenced success. A self-referenced mindset emphasizes your context, develops transferrable thought processes, and gives you the freedom to try things and fail positively.

Self-efficacy—the topic of Chapter 6—is the growth mindset applied to a specific task. *Self-efficacy is a fundamental ingredient to overcoming obstacles and achieving success.* Self-efficacy can be improved in numerous ways. The most effective are via personal experience and seeing someone you relate to do it. Other common but less effective ways of improving self-efficacy are social persuasion, physiological factors, visualization, and faith.

Our third Spotlight covered the 80/20 Rule, and how it applies to our training. Some of our behaviors are much more important than others, and we need to identify them and maximize them. Other behaviors take up more time and energy but provide less benefit. We need to minimize these. We can equate the relative importance of activities with the size of the arrows in our Momentum Model.

Finally, in Chapter 7, we discussed mental causation. *All behavior is caused. All causation is mental. We become what we think about most of the time.* We create "mental representations" for all of our behaviors. The better our mental representation, the better we will execute. Our passion and concentration determine the quality of our mental representations. The more we create habits of mind that boost and sustain our passion and concentration, the more likely we are to develop expert mental representations.

Recap of Part 2: Applying Our Effort Optimally

In Part 2 we switched gears from attitudes to effort. We discussed which areas we should maximize, which we should minimize, and the importance of mistakes, analysis, and perseverance. We also looked at Next Level 80/20, a tool for identifying the single most important area to focus your energy.

Chapter 8 was about goal setting: *Optimal training is centered on clear, executable goals. We train to improve specific abilities.* All experts in their fields get to that position via purposeful practice. Purposeful practice depends on high quality execution goals, intense concentration, immediate feedback, and a willingness to get out of our comfort zone. We also covered the difference between North Star goals and Next Step goals, and we looked at five ways to plan for North Star goals that make goal-setting more effective.

Our final Spotlight covered Next Level 80/20. When we apply the 80/20 rule to itself, we can narrow down even more the activities that make the most difference for our success. In doing so, we identified consistent effort as the Level 1 key factor, followed by purposeful practice at Level 2 and understanding the Hidden Training Program at Level 3.

Chapter 9 explored the concept of Discipline. *Certain behaviors, if practiced with consistent quality, ensure Optimal Training.* Many people fall victim to the Discipline Illusion, where they fail to build discipline into their routines because they imagine negative impacts that don't exist. We also introduced the idea of Systems—anything you do that sustains your positive momentum—and building them around your "lazy default" and a friction-less environment. You should create systems for any area of your life that contributes to your success but is not worth maximizing.

If we practice purposefully and have effective systems, the biggest remaining obstacle to our success will be mistakes, the topic of Chapter 10. *Making mistakes is an effective way to learn and improve.* We make mistakes of commission and omission. The most important are Striving mistakes, which occur when we push beyond our limits. We also introduced the idea of Risk and Performance Rewards, which shows why we benefit from being bold in our training and racing, as opposed to overly conservative or reckless.

Chapter 11 analyzed...analysis, with the following principle at the core: *Racing times and personal records indicate progress at one point in time.* Keeping a daily activity log and doing a monthly Momentum Model are effective tools for analyzing your progress. We also covered fundamental attribution errors, the "talent trap," and "non-constructive" criticism. These are difficult to avoid and we don't want them to distort how we think about our training.

In the final chapter, we discussed the importance of perseverance. *Optimal performances and realizing your potential are results of painstaking preparation and hard work.* In the short-term, it's important to build momentum by focusing on the few biggest forces affecting our training. In the longer-term, we need to give careful consideration to all the small forces that collectively push us or restrain us. We also covered injuries and the need to prepare for them mentally, both to avoid them and maximize our recovery from them.

These chapters were filled with tips and strategies for making improvements, big and small. As you engage with your training, take on more responsibility, adopt more Next Step goals and purposeful practice, build effective systems and identify 80/20 improvements to your life, you will build the positive feedback loops necessary to make a leap.

I hope you can return to this book continually for inspiration and practical tips to make not just one, but many leaps. I wish you my best, and hope to have provided a small positive external force to help you on your journey.

Optimal Everything

You have no doubt realized you can apply all these concepts to more than just running. The ideas are universal and transferrable. Running is simply a practical framework for discussing them.

You can apply these ideas to your studies, your job, your hobbies, raising children, traveling, gambling, volunteering, writing, learning languages, other sports, and pretty much any other endeavor.

After I engaged with these principles, I saw improvements everywhere: my grades, my efficiency at work, my writing, my decision-making, and my general happiness. I've used these principles to help me overcome difficulties with my marriage, learning new jobs, managing difficult colleagues, traveling the world with my family, and of course, writing this book.

They are not a cure-all by any means, and I am far (far far far) from perfect at implementing them. But these principles provide a proven framework for understanding and navigating whatever situation I am in. I have no doubt they can do the same for you.

If you would like to share with me what changes you've made (in your running or elsewhere) please send me an email at: maketheleapbook@gmail.com. I'd love to learn from you.

The Optimal Training Principles

1. *Your athletic performance is a result of your attitude, your effort, and your training methods*

2. *Active engagement in training makes the process more understandable, more relevant, and more effective. (And more fun.)*

3. *You are responsible for your own training.*

4. *Ability is a variable, not a constant. The harder you work, the more able you become.*

5. *Self-efficacy is a fundamental ingredient to overcoming obstacles and achieving success.*

6. *All behavior is caused. All causation is mental. We become what we think about most of the time.*

7. *Optimal training is centered on clear, executable goals. We train to improve specific abilities.*

8. *Certain behaviors, if practiced with consistent quality, ensure Optimal Training.*

9. *Making mistakes is an effective way to learn and improve.*

10. *Racing times and personal records indicate progress at one point in time.*

11. *Optimal performances and realizing your potential are results of painstaking preparation and hard work.*

Glossary

The following terms are defined as I use them within the book. These definitions may not align to a standard dictionary or Wikipedia entry. (Parentheses include the main chapter where they are discussed.)

4+2 Factors - in self-efficacy, there are four canonical factors: personal experience, vicarious experience, social persuasion, and physiological factors; I have added two more: visualization and faith (ch 6)

80/20 Rule - the idea that 80% of our results come from 20% of our activities; a simple tool for prioritizing our time and effort (80/20 Rule)

Ability - what we are able to do; the result of our talent and effort over time; changes over time (ch 5, ch 11)

Accountability - see "responsibility"

Analogy Approach - a technique for developing a Growth Mindset, in which you view improvement in a different area as evidence that the same can be true in the area you are interested in (ch 5)

Analysis - see "evaluation"

Arrows - used to represent forces in the Momentum Model; the size of the arrow represents the force's strength (Momentum Model, ch 12)

Attitude - the mental approach we take toward an activity (ch 2)

Attribution - the way in which we describe and explain our performance (Attribution Theory)

Attribution errors - see "fundamental attribution error" and "talent trap"

Attribution Theory - developed by Bernard Weiner, a theory that connects how individuals explain their performances (Attribution Theory)

Backcast - a strategy in which you imagine you have achieved a goal, and think backward to identify all the obstacles you had to overcome (ch 8)

Bold - acting aggressively but with a plan that accepts some amount of risk; this is the ideal attitude to take when entering a competition or challenge (ch 10)

Brushing your teeth - an example of a system that can be more or less complicated depending on the individual; please do it (ch 9)

Build Phase - the first phase of a Leap Cycle; in this phase improvement is minimal, but if the work being done is high quality it will lead to a leap (ch 1)

Build to Leap - a transition between the Build and Leap phases; we can tell our training is working, but improvement is still gradual (ch 1)

Causal dimensions - the three defining aspects of an attribution: locus of control (internal vs external), stability (fixed vs variable), and controllability (can we control it?) (Attribution Theory)

Causation - the act of causing a behavior or result; the driving force (ch 7)

Coaches - the people we delegate responsibility to for our training, and imitate when we get together with teammates after we graduate (ch 4)

Cognitive load - the mental effort being used during an activity (Ch 9)

Compounding - the result when improvements are fed back into a positive feedback loop, thus generating continually greater improvements with each cycle; if continued long enough, creates exponential growth and leaps (ch 1)

Concentration - see "focus"

Concrete - what all goals should be; achieved by telling others (ch 8)

Conservative - entering a race or competition unwilling to accept sufficient risk due to fearing the negative outcome more than desiring the positive outcome (ch 10)

Consideration - how much we have thought about a habit or behavior; habits tend to have been Never, Actively, or Previously considered (ch 9)

Consistency - repeating the same behaviors continuously over time; consistency is essential to creating a positive feedback loop and compounding (ch 1, ch 12)

Consistency bias - an innate bias in which we wish to act in accordance with what we have declared, or with who we believe ourselves to be (ch 7)

Controllability - whether or not we can influence the factor; requires the factor be internal and variable, which is typically Effort (Attribution Theory)

Criticism - a type of feedback in which your attitude or behaviors are judged to need improvement; often given bluntly and ineffectively (ch 11)

Declarative - see "explicit"

Deliberate Practice - the highest form of practice as defined by Anders Ericsson; it is purposeful practice with a world class coach (ch 8)

Digital cleanse - removing digital distractions from your environment, typically for a period of at least 2 weeks (ch 7)

Discipline bubble - finding one other person to work with you in establishing new disciplined behaviors; useful when your team environment is not conducive to the changes you wish to make (ch 9)

Discipline Illusion - the belief that maintaining a disciplined lifestyle is restrictive and exhausting; related to Discipline = Willpower Fallacy (ch 9)

Discipline = Willpower Fallacy - the belief that willpower is essential to maintaining discipline; related to Discipline Illusion (ch 9)

Disengagement - the loss or lack of passion or motivation, and the resulting lack of effort put into an activity (ch 3)

Distraction - anything that affects your ability to focus; what our environment is filled with (ch 7)

Effectiveness - how appropriate an activity is for your intended outcome (ch 2)

Efficiency - how well you do something, relative to the time and effort you put into it (ch 2)

Effort - the energy you apply toward an activity; one of the four factors of Attribution Theory; what high achievers attribute success and failure to; a central component of a growth mindset and self-efficacy (ch 2, ch 5, ch 6, Attribution Theory)

Engagement - what happens when passion meets motivation; the act of investing your mental energy into all aspects of your training; improves understanding and relevance; how we discover the Hidden Training Program (ch 3)

Environment - the surroundings in which you live and train; where positive and negative external forces exist in the Momentum Model; an area filled with triggers that can help or hurt your behavior (ch 9, Momentum Model)

Evaluation - reviewing your training to identify areas for improvement; one part of training that you are responsible for, along with your coach (ch 4)

Execution - the act of carrying out an activity; the quality of your execution determines the quality of your results (ch 4, ch 8)

Expectations - what we believe will happen in the future; these set the ceiling for our ability, so they must be set productively (Intro)

Explicit - actively thinking about something, especially routines (ch 7)

Exponential growth - the result of a positive feedback loop and consistent compounding; the vertical line in the Leap Phase of a Leap Cycle (ch 1)

Faith - the belief in a high power or purpose; often a source of self-efficacy for those who hold it (ch 6)

Fakers - someone who approaches an activity with concentration but not passion; they are typically going through the motions (ch 7)

Fartlek - the one, sole reason I didn't keep leaping; a legitimate word that spell check thinks isn't real; my current favorite type of workout (ch 4)

Feedback - the portion of your results that goes back into the process; what you hear from your coach or teammates that guides your training; can be explicit or implicit (ch 1, ch 6, ch 8, ch 11)

Feedback loop - a process in which some portion of the results are entered back into the process, which is repeated indefinitely (ch 1)

FIST - Facebook, Instagram, Snapchat and Twitter; the companies pounding you with non-stop distractions (ch 7)

Fixed - the quality of being unchanging; in Attribution Theory, talent and task difficulty are considered fixed factors (Attribution theory)

Fixed Mindset - coined by Carol Dweck; an attitude in which our talent determines our performance; it leads to a desire to demonstrate ability and a fear of taking on new challenges (ch 5)

Focus - the ability to block out distractions and think about one thing for an extended time; a critical component of building mental representations and purposeful practice (ch 7, ch 8)

Footnote - an opportunity for undisciplined authors to add irrelevant content, jokes, or personal anecdotes; they are my favorite

Force - anything acting on your Momentum Model; can be internal or external, positive or negative, strong or weak; represented by arrows (Momentum Model)

Formal Training Program - everything your coach or training program requires you to do (ch 3)

Fundamental Attribution Error - mistakenly attributing someone's behavior to their talent or personality, which are internal and fixed traits; a common mistake we make in evaluating behavior (ch 11)

Goal commitment - the act of publicly sharing your goals in order to reinforce your commitment to achieving them (ch 8)

Goal-setting - making a new goal; more important than the goal itself (ch 8)

Green's Razor - "Never attribute to talent or luck that which can be adequately explained by effort." (Attribution Theory)

Growth Mindset - coined by Carol Dweck; an attitude in which our effort determines our performance; it leads to a desire to learn and improve and embracing new challenges (ch 5)

Habits of thought - the consistent use of mental models and frameworks to explain situations and outcomes (ch 7, ch 12)

Hidden Training Program - what you REALLY need to do to be successful; includes all of the non-practice activities that make up our daily life (ch 3)

High achiever - someone who consistently performs up to their ability; typically attributes both success and failure to their effort (Attribution theory)

Hippo - a vicious grizzly bear killer and you know it, Andrew (ch 3)

Hot side of Mercury - see "surface of the sun"

Ice bath - a terrible invention that dedicated athletes use to increase their recovery; a place where skinny people go to suffer (ch 3)

Implicit - anything done unconsciously, especially routines (ch 7)

Improvement curve - what your improvement looks like when charted on a graph, typically takes an S-shape when a leap is visible (ch 1)

Keychain - an example of a "painful to sit on" environmental trigger that can lead to positive behavior (ch 9)

Law of Conservation of Mental Energy - "if we can do something without thinking, we will"; this explains why we fall into many bad habits (ch 7)

Lazy Default - what we do when we don't want to put energy into something; can be positive and productive or negative and unproductive; a key factor in understanding discipline and creating good systems (ch 9)

Leap - rapid and sustained improvement in one's performance (ch 1)

Leap Cycle - the three phases of a leap: Build, Leap, Sustain (ch 1)

Leap to Sustain - a transition between the Leap and Sustain phases; improvement slows and our performances begin to plateau (ch 1)

Linear (thinking/improvement) - the belief that improvement occurs in a straight line (Intro, ch 1)

Locus of Control - in Attribution theory, whether or not a factor is internal or external (Attribution theory)

Log - a book or diary in which you track your time, workouts, etc (ch 9, ch 11)

Low achiever - someone who performs below their ability; typically they do not attribute their success or failure to effort (Attribution theory)

Low hanging fruit - the low hanging fruit are easier to pick than the fruit at the top of the tree; in training, it is the activity that gets you the most benefit for the least effort (Intro)

Luck - anything that helps or hurts our progress that cannot be expected or planned for; one of the four causal dimensions (Attribution theory)

Make a leap - see "Leap"

Mental representation - coined by Anders Ericsson; "a mental structure that corresponds to an object, an idea, a collection of information, or anything else, concrete or abstract, that the brain is thinking about"; it is the way we define an activity in our minds; high achievers tend to have very well-defined mental representations (ch 7)

Mental model - a framework or way of thinking that explains the world (Intro)

Mental training - the act of training ourselves to think better (Intro)

Mentor - someone to guide you on your journey; find one, or even two (ch 12)

Mistake of commission - a mistake that resulted from a decision to act (ch 10)

Mistake of omission - a mistake that resulted from a failure to act (ch 10)

Momentum Model - a mental model in which we view our progress as a ball rolling up a hill, with internal/external positive/negative forces moving the ball and obstacles along the path to our goal (Momentum Model)

Motivation - the desire to achieve a goal; one of the key drivers of strong engagement (ch 3)

Mt. Fuji - a mountain with many paths to the top, but one everyone uses (ch 2)

Naive Practice - The idea that simply doing something repeatedly will lead to improvement (ch 8)

Next Level 80/20 - The result of applying the 80/20 rule on itself; doing so enables us to see that it is possible for 4% of our actions to create 2/3 of our results (Next Level 80/20)

Next Step goal - an execution-oriented goal focused on your activity in the moment; it is one of the key components of purposeful practice (ch 8)

Norm-referenced excellence - excellent performance judged against external standards (times) or other competitors (place) (ch 5)

North Star goal - a distant goal you hope to achieve in the future (ch 8)

Obstacles - Any event or challenge that slows your momentum; typically 3 kinds: preparation, perseverance, luck; a key component of the Momentum Model (Momentum Model, ch 12)

Optimal Training Principle - a core belief or reality that serves as the foundation for your training program; there are 11 in this book, each with a chapter dedicated to it

Passion - an intense interest, regardless of any particular outcome; an essential component of engagement and building mental representations (ch 3, ch 7)

Perseverance - the ability to continue in the face of obstacles, setbacks, and challenges (ch 12)

Persistence - see Perseverance

Personal experience - something you have done in the past; the strongest factor in creating strong self-efficacy (ch 6)

Personal limit - the maximum improvement you can make in the time period you are considering; your personal limit for this season will be lower than your personal limit for your career; also called "short-term potential" (ch 1)

Physiological factors - how you feel when you enter a situation (fear, stress, etc); one of the four canonical factors contributing to self-efficacy (ch 6)

Planning - according to Eisenhower, it is everything; see "preparation"

Positive feedback loop - a specific type of feedback loop that results in compounding improvement and exponential growth (ch 1)

Potential - the limit of your ability; differs in the near and long term; what athletes with a growth mindset are focused on achieving (ch 1, ch 12)

Pre-conditional rule - a rule that commits you to doing the preparation for the behavior you want (i.e. sitting at the desk with your book open for 5 minutes when you need to study) (ch 9)

Pre-Mortem - a practice whereby you assume you failed to achieve a goal and then tell the story of that failure; useful for identifying potential obstacles prior to starting a project or pursuing a goal (ch 8)

Preparation - the act of getting ready to do or deal with something; best when done painstakingly (ch 12)

Priorities - the areas in training or your life that are most important; where we should focus our effort when our results are not proportional (80/20 rule)

Procedural - see "implicit"

Proportional - a situation where the inputs and outputs are close to equal; our training activities are NOT proportional (80/20 Rule)

Purpose - the objective of an activity; something you must know prior to beginning if you are to execute efficiently (ch 8)

Purposeful Practice - a higher form of practice than Naive Practice, which requires focus on Next Step goals, immediate feedback, intense focus, and getting out of one's comfort zone (ch 8)

Quality - a measure of *how well* you do an activity; a key component in creating a Leap Cycle (ch 2)

Quantity - a measure of *how much* you do an activity (ch 2)

Rabbit - a runner who sets the pace in a race; also the foul beast that guards the Cave of Caerbannog (ch 10)

Reckless - an approach to competing that takes on high risk without planning; can lead to breakthroughs but often results in poor performances (ch 10)

Responsibility - holding yourself accountable for your performance; all athletes must be responsible for Planning, Execution, and Evaluation (ch 4)

Reframing Approach - a technique for developing a Growth Mindset, in which successful performances are actively attributed to effort and preparation (ch 5)

Risk - the potential downside of a plan or activity; something all athletes must accept if they are to achieve a breakthrough performance

Rule #1 of Communication - "most people aren't good at it" (ch 11)

Rule of Thumb - a simple, generic rule for a situation, something I used a little too often in this book to make my points (ch 2, ch 7, ch 9)

Self-efficacy - the belief in what you can achieve given the amount of effort you put into it; an essential factor in achieving greatness (ch 6)

Self-esteem - our feeling of self-worth; is not a relevant factor in achieving greatness (ch 6)

Self-referenced excellence - excellent performance judged against internal or personal standards, including our expectations or the situation (ch 5)

Shoelaces - things we use to tighten our shoes; must be tied (Intro)

Social persuasion - being told we can do something by someone we trust; one of the four factors that lead to high self-efficacy (ch 6)

Spotlight - a very short chapter illustrating a mental model or key idea, typically 3-5 pages long; there are four in this book: Momentum Model, Attribution Theory, 80/20 Rule, Next Level 80/20

Stability - whether or not a factor is fixed or variable; one of the causal dimensions in Attribution theory (Attribution Theory)

Striving Mistakes - mistakes we make because we are trying to do something for the first time; the best kind of mistakes to make (ch 10)

Surface of the sun - along with "hot side of Mercury," an ineffective idea to think about while suffering in an ice bath (ch 4)

Sustain Phase - the third and final phase in a Leap Cycle, a long slow period of moderate improvement after we make our leap; naturally turns into the next Build Phase when quality is improved (ch 1)

Systems - habits and routines we create that lead to positive outcomes with minimal effort required to execute them; the best strategy for "rest-of-80%" activities (ch 9)

Task Difficulty - how hard a task is; one of the four factors in Attribution Theory, external and fixed (Attribution Theory)

Talent - our innate ability, often tied to our potential; one of the four factors in Attribution Theory, internal and fixed (ch 5, Attribution Theory)

Talent Trap - a specific attribution error where we see a performance and assume it is primarily due to talent; often made with East African runners (ch 6)

Think Small, Think All - the attitude of identifying all of the small influences on your training and getting them to be positive (ch 12)

Time - a measure of *how long* you do an activity; a key aspect of a positive feedback loop and a Leap Cycle (ch 2)

Tomorrow's Key Three - a strategy of writing down your three top priorities for the next day and sharing them with someone to hold you accountable (ch 7)

Training Methods - part of the Optimal Training Pyramid, along with Attitude and Effort; the third and least important part (ch 2)

Trigger - anything that initiates a thought or behavior (ch 9)

Value check - in goal-setting, the strategy of imagining the lifestyle you will need to maintain to achieve your goal; if you cannot imagine sustaining that lifestyle, you should re-evaluate your North Star goal (ch 8)

Variable - changes over time; what someone with a Growth Mindset believes about their ability; a key dimension in Attribution Theory (Attribution Theory)

Vicarious experience - seeing someone you relate to accomplish something; the second-most powerful factor in establishing high self-efficacy (ch 6)

Vicious cycle - a positive feedback loop that results in a bad outcome (ch 1)

Virtuous cycle - a positive feedback loop that results in a good outcome (ch 1)

Visualization - a technique where we imagine how an activity will unfold before we attempt to do it; one of the factors that influences self-efficacy; Alex Honnold's super power (ch 6)

Willpower - the mental energy we have to apply to a problem; gets used up when we have to use it in our daily lives; best conserved for purposeful practice; mistakenly believed to be essential to a disciplined life (ch 7, ch 9)

Zzzzz - onomatopoeia for sleep, something you should get more of (ch 9)

Acknowledgements

First and foremost, I want to thank Samantha Carrell for her assistance in all areas of this project. I frequently found myself stuck and not making progress, and her support is what got me over the finish line. From editing to formatting to publishing to marketing, she helped me create and execute on the plan. She was a bona fide Next Level 80/20 force.

This book wouldn't have been possible if not for the many amazing coaches I was fortunate to train under. Bob Grove was my first running coach. He was a science teacher and cross country coach at Littlerock High School. He joined the school two years before I did, and the team had 8 members. By my junior year, we won the Golden League Title and under his guidance I twice qualified for the California State Championships.

If this book comes off as critical of my high school training's sophistication, it is because I still had so much to learn when I arrived at UCLA. But I loved running for Coach Grove and it was his comment in the van coming back from Santa Cruz my sophomore year that made me believe I could be one of the best runners in the league. With just fifteen words he changed how I thought of myself.

He is also the best teacher I had at any level.

Bruce Galler was my track coach for two years at Littlerock High School. I still remember fondly doing intervals where the last one was always "guts." He not only helped me to run fast enough to get noticed by colleges, he also taught me about music, traveling, and being myself.

Mike Fluharty coached me for my senior year and was a dedicated coach to our entire distance squad. I struggled with obligations, injuries and inconsistency that year, but I still ran close to my personal bests with his guidance.

Bob Larsen offered me a spot at UCLA and played a pivotal role in my learning how to train. It was later that I really appreciated the lessons he was teaching me, as at the time I'm not sure I was mature enough to fully adopt them.

I love that Bob continues to join us for our Alumni 2400 meet on the day of the UCLA-USC dual meet, and his post-season "Chocolate Malt 2-mile" and "Diddy Reece 800m" races were where I ran some of my lifetime personal bests. To this day he is one of my favorite people to speak with, and his humility and generosity are unparalleled.

Eric Peterson was my coach my final two years at UCLA and helped to guide me to my best performances. I believe we found each other at just the right time. I needed someone of his intensity, confidence, and inspiration. And he needed someone to step into a leadership role on the team. I love his infectious laugh, his vertical hand clap, and the passion he brought to every workout.

Helen Lehman-Winters was the assistant coach for my final two years at UCLA and she brought a warmth to our team that made it easier for all of us to train at our best. It is essential to know that your coach is there for you as you put yourself out there, and she was always there. I am so impressed at what she has accomplished and she deserves every success she's earned.

I hope this book honors them sufficiently, as I feel blessed to have been an athlete under their guidance.

I also wish to thank the many friends and colleagues who read draft versions of this book. Scott Abbott and Ashley Cibelli provided invaluable feedback throughout the process and helped to get the book into its final format. Joe Green, Mason Moore, and Devin Elizondo identified countless areas for improvement and I can't adequately thank them for the time they put into reading it. Josh Briggs, Sam Burke, Christian Cushing-murray, Jason Lewis,

Robert Lusitana, Jon Rankin and Ken Reeves all provided insight, suggestions and support.

A huge thank you to Nadine Denten, who did the cover art-work and assisted me with countless aspects of the book launch. I introduce her to everyone as "a wizard" and that's exactly what she is. She makes things look awesome and she makes things work. And always with a smile!

To my wife, Rika, thank you for supporting me and bearing with me on all the mornings and evenings I chose to work on this. Your support was invaluable.

Lastly, thank you to *all of you* who read this book. Please do connect with me and tell me what you thought.

About the Author

Bryan Green is the co-founder of Go Be More apparel, where he also co-hosts the Go Be More Podcast. He lives in Sendai, Japan with his wife and two daughters. Prior to moving to Japan he used the same mindset in this book to excel in his career at Apple and to learn Japanese and Italian as an adult.

He competed at UCLA from 1997 to 2002, and was a two-time individual qualifier to the NCAA Cross Country Championships in 2000 and 2001.

HS bests (3rd fastest time*)
800m: 1:59 (2:00)
1600m: 4:23 (4:26)
3200m: 9:22 (9:29)
XC (3mi): 15:17 (15:35)

Collegiate bests
1500m: 3:50.1 (3:52)
5000m: 14:19 (14:22)
10000m: 29:25 (29:40)
XC (8k): 23:57 (24:11)

*My teammate Scott Abbott used to argue that one's 3rd fastest time is a more accurate reflection of their actual ability. I agree.

maketheleapbook@gmail.com
maketheleapbook.com
@maketheleapbook
gobemore.co

Get my newsletter!

Sign up at maketheleapbook.com/newsletter

Learn More

Think Better Workbook
I created this hands-on, practical companion guide to help runners implement the key principles we discuss in Make the Leap. If you are an athlete looking to take your mental training to the next level, this will help you. If you are a coach, it will offer you a simple framework for discussing these principles with your team.

Get yours at MakeTheLeapBook.com - Enter the code "THINKBETTER20" at checkout to receive your 20% discount.

Go Be More Apparel
I believe strongly in filling our environment with concrete representations of our goals. Whether it's athletic gear for your workouts or casual wear for your day-to-day, we want our apparel to be that physical reminder for you as you Go Be More.

Check us out at GoBeMore.co - Enter the code "MAKETHELEAPBOOK20" at checkout to receive a 20% discount.

Go Be More Podcast
My podcast with Go Be More co-founder Jon Rankin is a place where we highlight inspiring stories from people who Go Be More in their daily lives. We've had hall-of-fame coaches, Olympians, Paralympians, Performers and Entrepreneurs, including Bob Larsen, Kara Goucher, Abdi Abdirahman, Khadevis Robinson, Tracy Sundlun, Amby Burfoot and many others. And we occasionally dive deep on a topic for getting more out of life in our conversation episodes.

Give us a listen at gobemore.co/gobemorepodcast